SHAKESPEARE AND THE SEA

The Mariners Mirrour

SHAKESPEARE
AND THE SEA

BY LIEUTENANT/COMMANDER

ALEXANDER FREDERICK FALCONER

V.R.D., M.A.

ROYAL NAVAL RESERVE

FREDERICK UNGAR PUBLISHING CO

NEW YORK

PRINTED IN GREAT BRITAIN BY
RICHARD CLAY AND COMPANY LTD
BUNGAY SUFFOLK

CONTENTS

Introduction	xi
The Sea as a Bulwark	1
The Royal Navy	3
A Naval Expedition	7
Sea Defeat	13
Ceremonial Visits at Sea	18
Aboard Pompey's Vessel	18
Pericles	20
Additional Ceremony	22
Sea Burial	24
Succour Ships	26
Mobilisations	28
A Royal Fleet Puts to Sea	30
Putting to Sea	32
Storms	35
The Tempest	36
Storms in *Pericles*	40
Sea and Sky	42
Shipwreck	44
Pirates	47
Pirates and Privateers	50
Officers Belonging to a Royal Ship	53
Seamen and Boys	63
Seamen	63
Boys	66
Sailors and Sea-soldiers	68
Pillage	71
Tides	73
The Stand	74
Eddies	75
Wind and Tide	75
Trinity House	78
Pilots	79
Dangers to Navigation	82

Sounding   86
Navigational Instruments   89
    Dials   90
    Globes and Maps   91
Sailing by the Star   93
Types of Ship   97
    Warships   97
    Ship's Boats   98
    Merchant Vessels   99
    Small Craft   100
Anchors and Cables   103
The Parts of a Ship   105
    Helm and Rudder   107
    Rigging   108
    Rope   110
    Masts   110
    Oars   111
    Ribs   112
    Sails   113
Gunnery   117
    Hamlet   122
Waves   124
Waterspouts   126
Promontories   127
Fishermen   129
Swimming   133
    Clarence's Dream   135
Seabirds and Waterfowl   137
    Creatures of the Deep   138
Signs of the Weather   140
    Winds   142
    Fog   143
Clouds   145
Epilogue   147
Appendix   151
A Tomb by the Seashore   151
A Blessing for one Born at Sea   151
Profane Oaths   153

FOREWORD

To Admiral Sir York Beverley a debt is acknowledged for the training he gave to officers of the Royal Naval Volunteer Reserve serving under his command aboard H.M.S. *Sussex* in the First and Fourth Cruiser Squadrons during the Second World War. Without it, this book could not have been written.

Acknowledgements for their courtesies are made to the librarians and trustees of the Admiralty Library, the National Maritime Museum, the Public Record Office, the British Museum, the Bodleian Library, Oxford, the Pepysian Library at Magdalene College, Cambridge, the National Library of Scotland, the Library of the University of St. Andrews, the Library of Trinity House, the Bibliothèque Nationale, Paris, and also to Dr. Louis B. Wright, the Director of the Folger Shakespeare Library, Washington.

For his interest in the work at all stages and for reading the manuscript, it is a pleasure to thank Mr. Ben Glazebrook.

INTRODUCTION

The defeat of the Spanish Armada in 1588 is so often thought of as a single, tremendous and final event that it has been allowed to overshadow the struggle that led up to it and that went on for fifteen years after. At the time, it could not have been viewed in such a way, and what is now acclaimed as the vanquishing of Spain is described as no more than "A defensive, but a victorious action",[1] in the table of expeditions between 1585 and 1603 drawn up by Admiral Monson who took part in most of them.

It has to be kept in mind that Shakespeare lived through a long-drawn-out naval war which lasted for eighteen years. Fears of invasion, the fitting out of ships, expeditions and seafights were part of the life of the time. State papers and Acts of Parliament, proclamations and edicts, tracts and news sheets, diaries and private correspondence disclose unending vigilance accompanied by constant rumours, alarms and crises. London, the capital and seat of the Court, the greatest seaport in the country, was the centre of all the tension and excitement. There, policy was framed as ambassadors and statesmen, admirals and generals came and went, and scientists, scholars, inventors, craftsmen, bankers and merchants assisted in their several ways all that was being done to ensure national safety.

That Shakespeare, on coming to London to take up his new career as a dramatist, brought with him knowledge of the sea and of the navy can be seen in his earliest plays. He was the first to bring the Royal Navy or "Navy Royal" into drama and in this, as in so much else, he has remained unapproached. In London, he had every chance to keep up his knowledge and even to add to it, for as a scene of maritime power it impressed all observers. An official visitor from Venice recorded in 1596:

"The Queen has every opportunity to muster fleets, for not only are all the ports of England full of ships, but especially the

[1] *The Naval Tracts of Sir William Monson*, edited by M. Oppenheim, Navy Records Society, Vol. III (1913), p. 326.

Thames, which from London to the sea measures some forty
or fifty Italian miles, where one sees nothing but ships and
seamen."[1]

Receptions were given aboard royal ships as they lay at anchor
in the river; scholars and mathematicians put to sea in them to
test their theories; potentates and their suites took passage in
them. Monson's notes show that many had these privileges in
warships: "There were divers English Lords and others that
passed with me by warrant also, which I have not set down because they concern not his Majesty's service so particularly."[2] In
such suites or groups Shakespeare may, from time to time, have
found himself, and he may often have been aboard royal ships
when they were in harbour.

Shakespeare's interest in the navy and in the sea held him
throughout his life. The greatest of dramatists remained pro-
foundly impressed and influenced by the greatest naval tradition
the world has seen. The manning and running of royal ships and
the ceremony observed in them; the duties of officers and seamen
and their characteristics, qualities and ways; strategy and the
principles of sea warfare, gunnery, grappling and boarding are
all known to him; so, too, are the main types of ship, their build,
rigging, masts, sails, anchors and cables. The sea itself in its
varied working, tides, waves, currents, storms and calms, never
goes out of his work. He draws on all this knowledge with great
ease and readiness, not only in making incidents and characters
true to life but in nautical imagery and figures of speech. That
he should know something of seamanship is more significant
than his acquaintance with navigation for, as late as 1623,
Sir Henry Mainwaring in introducing his *Seaman's Dictionary*
or *Nomenclator Navalis*, the first of its kind to appear, remarks
"To understand the art of navigation is far easier learned than to
know the practice and mechanical working of ships, with the
proper terms belonging to them, in respect that there are helps
for the first by many books, which give easy and ordinary rules
for the obtaining to it; but for the other, till this, there was not so
much as a means thought of, to inform any one in it."[3] But this

---

[1] *Elizabethan England*, by E. M. Tenison, Vol. X (1953), p. 174.   [2] Monson, III, 77–78.

[3] *The Life and Works of Sir Henry Mainwaring*, edited by G. E. Manwaring and W. G. Perrin,
Navy Records Society, Vol. II (1922), p. 85. *Works* written between 1620 and 1623 and first
printed in 1644.

Shakespeare does know, and he must have learned it at first hand. Moreover, only a detailed glossary could do justice to the extent and accuracy of his use of sea terms.

Navigation was of national concern. There was good reason, it was held, to give it first place in the arts and sciences for, "by the use and practice thereof . . . is the Navy Royal furnished, the Realme fortified, and the commonwealth enriched".[1] A great era which was to see developments of the most far-reaching kind had begun. Hakluyt, who was teaching cosmography at Oxford "to the singular pleasure, and generall contentment"[2] of his hearers, again and again urged Walsingham to found a lectureship in navigation in London and one in mathematics at Oxford, maintaining that in his "simple judgement" it would prove to be the best hundred pounds "that was bestowed these five Hundred yeares in England".[3] Drake, "in most bountiful manner", had earlier offered to help.[4] But, in the end, it was left to the citizens of London to do what was needed. Fearing that the Spaniards, after their defeat, might make another attempt, they instituted a lectureship in navigation in November 1588 as part of a scheme for the defence of the city and kingdom. Thomas Hood, who had been providing instruction privately, was appointed. His inaugural address was a reminder of dangers past, "We have seene them on our coaste, and heard the thunder of their shot," and also a call to prepare for what might lie ahead by giving increased attention to navigation, hydrography, astronomy, geometry and geography. The lectures were attended not only by men under training but by "all other whome it pleased to resort".[5]

At Gresham College, endowed by Sir Thomas Gresham, founder of the Royal Exchange, and opened in 1598, astronomy was one of the principal subjects. Sunset and clear night skies bring into view a universe that cannot be seen by day, and this vast world overhead enables ships far out at sea to find their way. The lectures, therefore, were to deal with "the principle of the sphere, and the theoriques of the planets, and the use of the astrolabe and the staf, and other common instruments for the

---

[1] *The Safeguard of Sailers*, by Robert Norman (1590); Epistle Dedicatory (1st edition, 1584).
[2] *The Principal Navigations Voyages Traffiques and Discoveries of the English Nation*, by Richard Hakluyt, Vol. I (1903), xviii.
[3] Hakluyt to Walsingham (1 April 1584). *Calendar of State Papers, Domestic Series*, 12/170, No. 1.
[4] Hakluyt, *Divers Voyages* (1582), "Epistle Dedicatorie".
[5] A COPIE OF THE SPEACHE: MADE by the *Mathematicall Lecturer, unto the Worshipfull Companye present* . . . T. HOOD (1588).

capacity of mariners".[1] Gresham's deed of gift stressed the importance of instruction that was practical and directed the professors to remember that, as those who listened to them would be mariners, merchants, and other citizens, the lectures should not be given "after the manner of the universities", but in a way that would best suit "the good liking and capacity of the said auditory".

In addition to lectures, there was a flow of books on navigation, astronomy, cartography, mathematics and geography from 1570 onwards.[2] Most of the writers made it clear in their prefaces that they hoped to win interest and had tried to present their subjects in a way that would be easy to follow. Blundeville's zeal for navigation was such that in the preface to his *Exercises*, he earnestly besought "all young Gentlemen to take these my simple pamphlets no lesse thankfully than they have done my horse booke, and in so doing I shall have just cause to thinke my labour well bestowed".[3]

Craftsmen lent their aid by bringing the making of globes, dials, astrolabes and other instruments to a high state of accuracy and finish. The Molyneux globes are of unrivalled workmanship and, in the production of maps and charts, engravers and printers showed remarkable skill.

The most famous publication was *The Mariners Mirrour* which appeared in 1588. Lord Howard of Effingham, Lord High Admiral of England, laid before the Privy Council, the Latin version of the Dutch *Spieghel der Zeevaerdt* by Wagenaer, with a request that an English translation be authorised. Anthony Ashley was commissioned to do it, but the English version was no mere translation. It was "fitted with necessarie additions for the use of Englishmen". Improvements were made in the charts, much information about harbours, roadsteads and soundings was added, there were sketches of the coast line and also of ships and small craft, and tribute was paid to the recent achievements of Drake and Howard. The frontispiece was of singular elegance.

Hakluyt fired the imagination of the venturesome and stirred the patriotism of all in his great compilation *The Principall Navigations, Voiages and Discoveries of the English nation*, 1589, and

[1] *The Lives of the Professors of Gresham College*, by John Ward, 2 vols., 1740, I, viii.
[2] *The Art of Navigation in England in Elizabethan and Early Stuart Times*, by David W. Waters (1958), pp. 127 ff.
[3] *M. Bundevilel His Exercises*, by Thomas Blundeville (1597). (To the Reader.)

in the revised edition of 1598–1600 he included the latest aid to accurate navigation, Edward Wright's epochmaking *Map of the World* which Shakespeare calls "the new map with the augmentation of the Indies".

Daring and dauntlessness were not confined to the voyagers who had earned a place in Hakluyt's pages. The spirit was widespread and this comes out strikingly in "The most dangerous and memorable adventure of Richard Ferris", 1590.[1] Ferris, a messenger of Her Majesty's Chamber, and two of his friends, one being a pilot of "sufficient skill and approved experience", rowed and sailed in a small wherry from London round the south coast to Bristol, with "safe return, contrary to the expectation of sundry persons". The dangers and difficulties they ran into were very much like those that go with ocean voyaging; currents, squalls, rough seas and storms; hazards from rocks and shoals; a narrow escape from pirates "who made towards us amain, meaning doubtless to have robbed us"; mishaps and accidents aboard: "my companion and oarfellow, Andrew Hill, in taking down our sail, fell overboard into the sea where, by great good hap, and by means that he held fast to a piece of our sail, we recovered him".

The venture created much interest. They were *fêted* at several places along the coast as they went, welcomed on board Her Majesty's ships at Plymouth and received with rejoicing at Bristol.

> "And on the next morning, the people gathered themselves together, and had prepared trumpets, drums, fifes and ensigns to go before the boat; which was carried upon men's shoulders round about the city, with the Waits of the said city playing orderly, in honour of our rare and dangerous attempt achieved.
>
> Afterwards, we were had to Master Mayor's, to the Aldermen's and Sheriffs' houses; where we were feasted most royally, and spared for no cost, all the time that we remained there."

Finally they returned to London where their entertainment was "great and honourable; especially at the Court".

The spirit in which it was undertaken is notable, for Ferris hoped that, as he himself "was never trained up on the water", his

[1] *An English Garner*, by Edward Arber, Vol. VI (1883), pp. 153 ff.

exploit might show the way and encourage his countrymen "to practise an ordinary passage through the like dangers, in such small wherry boats; especially when necessary occasion shall serve, the better to daunt the enemies of this nation; who in such flaws and frets at sea, dare not hazard their galleys to go forth, though they be of far greater force to brook the seas".

Enthusiasm for feats of navigation and seamanship is also seen in the veneration shown for Drake's ship the *Golden Hind* on board which he was knighted by the Queen on returning from his voyage round the world in 1581. "What a wonder we made of Sir Francis Drake's vessel", exclaimed Pepys long afterwards.[1] It was laid up in a kind of dry dock at Deptford and was visited year after year by crowds of sightseers. By degrees, it fell into decay, this being hastened latterly by hunters for keepsakes who allowed themselves much freedom, and in the reign of Charles II, it was broken up. But from a part of the hull a chair was made and presented to the University of Oxford.

> To this great ship which round the globe has run
> And matched in race the chariot of the sun . . .
> In her new shape this sacred port allow.

> Drake and his ship could not have wished from fate,
> A more blest station or more blest estate,
> For, lo! a seat of endless rest is given,
> To her in Oxford, and to him in Heaven.[2]

Advances in navigation, sea warfare, exploration, discovery dominated the life of Shakespeare's age and are reflected throughout his work. Even the problems that colonising was to bring are confronted by him in the *Tempest*.

---

[1] *Samuel Pepys's Naval Minutes*, edited by J. R. Tanner, Navy Records Society (1926), p. 85.
[2] (Abraham Cowley, 1618/77.)

THE SEA AS A BULWARK

"England bound in with the triumphant sea"

In his *Defence of the Realme*, 1596,[1] Sir Henry Knyvett, like other Elizabethans, extolled the sea as the bulwark of the kingdom.

> "For the first poynt, it maie briefelie and trulie be saide, that it is an Islande environed with a large Sea . . . replenished with a puissant Navye, as well Royall as of Marchantes and others, and so both naturallie and artificiallie fenced and fortified with a most strong ditch and mighty wall, as thoughe God in his gratious wisedome had predestinated it ever to remaine invincible."

But Shakespeare has given finest expression to that spirited patriotism which delighted to think of the island, "girt in with the ocean",[2] as inviolable by Divine decree. It comes into the earliest of the plays:

> Let us be backed with God and with the seas
> Which He hath given for fence impregnable.   *3 Hen. VI* 4.1.43

It continues in *King John*:

>   that pale, that white faced shore,
> Whose foot spurns back the ocean's roaring tides
> And coops from other lands her islanders,
> . . . that England, hedged in with the main,
> That water-walled bulwark, still secure
> And confident from foreign purposes.   2.1.23

And it finds fullest and most inspiring utterance in the speech of John of Gaunt:

> This royal throne of kings, this sceptered isle,
> This earth of majesty, this seat of Mars,
> This other Eden, demi-paradise,
> This fortress built by nature for herself
> Against infection and the hand of war,
> This happy breed of men, this little world,
> This precious stone set in the silver sea,

---

[1] Tudor and Stuart Library (1906).   [2] *3 Hen. VI* 4.8.20.

> Which serves it in the office of a wall,
> Or as a moat defensive to a house,
> Against the envy of less happier lands—
> This blessed plot, this earth, this realm, this England.
>   *Rich. II* 2.1.40

It is heard still in the last plays, though in a new way, no longer in flights of oratory but in the sharp exchanges of angry and scornful debate. Indeed, two of the baser characters in *Cymbeline* appear for the time being in a better light because of a sudden upsurge of patriotism that makes them repudiate the right of a foreign power to exact tribute:

>   Britain is
> A world by itself, and we will nothing pay
> For wearing our own noses.   *Cymb.* 3.1.13

Defiance rests once more on confidence in the impregnable position of the island:

>   ribbed and paled in
> With rocks unscaleable and roaring waters,
> With sands that will not bear your enemies' boats
> But suck them up to th' topmast.   3.1.20

It is kept up in the challenge that comes at the end, with its Churchillian ring:

>   if you seek us afterwards in other terms,
> you shall find us in our salt-water girdle: if you
> beat us out of it, it is yours: if you fall in the
> adventure, our crows shall fare the better for you:
> and there's an end.   3.1.80

THE ROYAL NAVY

"Our Royal Fleet"

When Sir Henry Knyvett spoke of England as "replenished with a puissant Navye as well Royall as of Marchantes and others", he took note of a distinction that Shakespeare is always careful to observe. He keeps these two contrasted types of sea service apart, and his interest in them both continues from the first plays to the last. Royal fleets are introduced in *Henry VI* and the world of merchant shipping in the *Comedy of Errors*.

Ships of the Royal Navy, then as now, were designed and manned as warships. The navy had its own organisation and officer structure, its law and custom and its strictly observed ceremony. Basic seamanship and navigation and much nautical language were the same in all ships, royal and merchant alike, but the navy, from the nature of its work in seeking out and engaging the enemy, its sea fights, chases, boardings, convoys, assaults and landings, and also its special task of exploring uncharted waters, was concerned with manoeuvres, strategy and armament and with complexities of navigation and seamanship in a way that the merchantman was not. Merchant ships had to be ready to defend themselves against attack, and they could be taken over in time of war, but their chief business was to proceed by the shortest route from one port to another.

The commanding officer of a warship was known as the Captain.[1] He was a fighting officer. Seamanship and navigation came under the Master, a professional mariner.

Sea warfare is brought into all three parts of *Henry VI*. Expeditions cross the seas "from England into France" as they have done age after age. Convoys are organised:

> These soldiers shall be levied
> And thou, Lord Bourbon, our high admiral
> Shall *waft*[2] them over with our royal fleet. 3 *Hen. VI* 3.3.251

and the last phase of a minor naval action is shown taking place.

---

[1] See p. 53.   [2] *waft* means convoy.

3

The scene is off the coast of Kent, the noise of a sea fight is heard, ordnance goes off, and a Lieutenant who is in command of a pinnace which "anchors in the Downs" after taking a prize, comes ashore in the long-boat with his prisoners, accompanied, as is correct, by a Master and Master's Mate. With him are Whitmore and a few soldiers. His opening speech shows him to be of some learning and this is fitting, for "a lieutenant is an employment for a gentleman well bred".[1] What he says has echoes of Seneca and is in keeping with the ominous atmosphere of the lone beach at nightfall, the dismal forebodings of the prisoners and the overwrought feelings of all.

> The gaudy, blabbing, and remorseful day
> Is crept into the bosom of the sea;
> And now loud-howling wolves arouse the jades
> That drag the tragic melancholy night;   2 *Hen. VI* 4.1.1.ff.

A summary trial is held:

> Therefore bring forth the soldiers of our prize,
> For whilst our pinnace anchors in the Downs
> Here shall they make their ransom on the sand,
> Or with their blood stain this discoloured shore.   4.1.8.ff.

He is unyielding as he recalls "The lives of those which we have lost in fight", and in this is supported by Whitmore in true sea phrase:

> I lost mine eye in *laying the prize aboard,*   1.25

The Lieutenant is a patriot. He breaks out in a long impassioned speech full of accusations and reproaches against the Duke of Suffolk whose disguise has been uncovered. Sentence is given with the authority of a commanding officer:

> Convey him hence, and on our long-boat's side
> Strike off his head.   1.68

Suffolk's demand,

> I charge thee waft me safely 'cross the Channel,   1.115

is met with mockery and scorn, and he is led off, hurling at his captors and self-appointed judges the taunt of "pirates".

From a few lines in Hall's *Chronicle*, Shakespeare has created a complete scene. In doing this, he not only adds much to his source, but corrects what he takes from it, or makes it more precise. The chronicler speaks of a "shippe of warre" and "the capitayne of the same barke", but Shakespeare, understanding

---

[1] *The Naval Tracts of Sir William Monson*, edited by M. Oppenheim, Navy Records Society, Vol. IV (1913), p. 16. The Folio reading "Lieutenant" is very important. See pp. 54–56.

the duties of a lieutenant and deciding to bring one in, rightly puts him in charge of a pinnace, and shows him exercising the powers of a captain as his rank entitled him to do. Suffolk tries to be contemptuous:

> Small things make base men proud: this villain here,
> Being captain of a pinnace, threatens more
> Than Bargulus the strong Illyrian pirate.   1.105

The Lieutenant is addressed as "captain" by his men because he is supplying the place of one. A cock boat is mentioned in the chronicle, but Shakespeare substitutes long-boat, the largest of a ship's boats, knowing that a company like this, leaving the pinnace in a cock boat, would never have reached shore.

Not the least important of his additions is the correct use of sea terms.

The *Comedy of Errors*, in contrast to *Henry VI*, ntroduces merchant shipping, "wealth increased by prosperous voyages", trade war, "goods confiscate", and reprisals.[1] The scene of the play is a great seaport with its harbour traffic, traders and voyagers who "hire waftage".

> Go, hie thee presently, post to the *road*,
> And if the wind *blow* any way from shore,
> I will not *harbour* in this town tonight,
> If any *bark put forth*, come to the mart.   3.2.148

A merchant, bound for Persia, lacks guilders for his voyage (4.1.4). A ship, ready to put to sea, well provisioned, stays

> but till her owner comes *aboard*,
> And then she *bears away* . . . Our *fraughtage*, sir,
> I have conveyed aboard, and I have bought
> The oil, the balsamum, and aqua-vitae . . .
> The *ship is in her trim*, the merry wind
> Blows fair from land: they stay for nought at all,
> But for their owner, master, and yourself.   4.1.87

At many critical turns, wind and tide and waiting ships add to the complications and excitements and heighten the tension. The sea also gives colour to the talk of the characters. Men are "Lords of the wide world and wild watry seas" (2.1.21). One of the brothers, in his apparently hopeless search for the other, sees himself as:

> a drop of water,
> That in the ocean seeks another drop,   1.2.34

[1] See also p. 44.

and Adriana, pleading the quality and constancy of her affections, draws the same likeness:

> as easy mayst thou fall
> A drop of water in the breaking gulf,
> And take unmingled thence that drop again,
> Without addition, or diminishing,
> As take from me thyself and not me too.   2.2.125

The setting and manner owe much to the ease and exactness with which nautical terms are used.

A NAVAL EXPEDITION

Othello

In the Italian story which gave Shakespeare an outline for the plot of his play, the voyage of Othello and his company to Cyprus is mentioned only in passing: "he embarked on board the galley with his wife and all his troops, and setting sail, they pursued their voyage, and with a perfectly tranquil sea arrived safely at Cyprus".[1] It was calm and uneventful. But instead of this, Shakespeare makes it "a stubborn and boisterous expedition", and creates a number of scenes which include the alarms, the conferences, the tactics, the stress of weather and finally the celebrations that mark the course of a hazardous but successful naval campaign. Indeed, the naval officer of the twentieth century can have little difficulty in recognising, even in its Elizabethan and Jacobean setting, a familiar world of intelligence reports, fleet orders, signals, strategy, manoeuvres and royal naval ceremony.

"It is a business of some heat", and begins, fittingly, with an alarm in the night requiring the "haste-post-haste appearance, even on the instant" of Othello who is to be commander in chief. Darkness adds to the tension. Messages from ships at sea pour in. The galleys

> Have sent a dozen sequent messengers
> This very night at one another's heels; 1.2.40

A council, hastily summoned, begins to weigh up the dangers as had been done when the Armada was known to be shaping course for England. Conflicting reports are considered dispassionately: "My letters say, a hundred and seven galleys";—"And mine, two hundred". But despite these differences, one thing is beyond doubt:

> yet do they all confirm
> A Turkish fleet, and bearing up to Cyprus. 1.3.6

Action must be taken on that.

---

[1] A New Variorum Edition, *Othello* (1886), p. 378.

When strategy is being decided, an unbroken flow of naval intelligence is vital and this is brought in by a chain of messengers. A sailor, with the traditional call "What, ho! what, ho! what, ho!", runs up and reports: "The Turkish preparation makes for Rhodes". This is contrary to earlier findings and, when examined, is dismissed as worthless:

> This cannot be,
> By no assay of reason: 'tis a pageant
> To keep us in false gaze.   1.3.17

The sound judgement of the council is confirmed by the next messenger who brings more news of the enemy's moves, and discloses their stratagem. "Steering with due course toward the isle of Rhodes", they have joined another fleet "of thirty sail";

> and now they do re-stem
> Their backward course, bearing with frank appearance
> Their purposes toward Cyprus.   1.3.37

The ruse is plain, final decisions are taken and Othello is put in charge. This was a stratagem of the time and it was not unusual for English squadrons to mislead the Spaniards by similar bold alterations of course.[1]

The next phase of the expedition is a storm at sea. Official papers constantly refer to plans delayed and strategy upset by "violent storms and seas mightily growne", and Seymour wrote to Walsyngham on 12 July 1588 that the Spaniards were "as greatly dangered by the raging seas as with their enemies".[2] "The wind-shaked surge with high and monstrous mane" is described by watchers on land, and there can be few scenes that succeed in conveying a sense of looking out to sea in a storm with such directness and vividness as this. "It is a high-wrought flood." Eager scanning of the horizon goes on: "What from the cape can you discern at sea?" and it is accompanied by a stream of comment from those keeping watch. "I never did like molestation view On the enchafed flood." And:

> What ribs of oak, when mountains melt on them,
> Can hold the mortise?   2.1.1 ff.

Thoughts turn to the progress of the war. "What shall we hear of this?" Surmises are made:

---

[1] *An English Garner*, edited by Edward Arber, Vol. VII, "The Commentaries of Sir Francis Vere", p. 100.

[2] *State Papers Relating to the Defeat of the Spanish Armada Anno 1588*, edited by John L. Laughton, Navy Records Society, Vol. I (1894), p. 254.

> If that the Turkish fleet
> Be not enshelter'd and embay'd, they are drown'd;
> It is impossible they bear it out.

Hardly is this said than a report proves it right: "News, lads! our wars are done." The fate of the enemy has been settled by the storm:

> The desperate tempest hath so bang'd the Turks,
> That their designment halts: a noble ship of Venice
> Hath seen a grievous wreck and sufferance
> On most part of their fleet.   2.1.20

Shakespeare is not falling back on coincidence here. This was frequent in sea warfare and what happens to the Turks is not unlike what had overtaken part of the Spanish fleet off the Irish coast.

> "For, assailed by a great storm in that sea, which so often is treacherous, some of their ships were driven on to the coast of that island between north and west, striking the reefs and breakers with dire results to the lives of all those on board and for many leagues, here, there and everywhere, were to be seen the remains of broken and shattered wreckage around that hostile coast."[1]

The account of this expedition would not be complete without the return of the victors to harbour and this is shown with the important addition of naval ceremony. The storm has scattered the ships and they are not returning in company. This, again, was not unusual, and one plea runs: "If our comming home scattering be objected, wee must plead the violence of stormes, against which no fore directions, nor present industry can prevaile."[2] The arrival of the first ship is reported: "The ship is here put in", 2.1.25, and then there is concern for the safety of Othello. His lieutenant says, "I have lost him on a dangerous sea". But, though "they were parted With foul and violent tempest", there are good grounds for hope:

> His bark is stoutly timbered, and his pilot
> Of very expert and approved allowance;   2.1.47

Excitement increases, "every minute is expectancy Of more arrivance", and when a second ship is sighted, the age old cry goes up:

> "a sail, a sail!"

[1] *The Naval Miscellany*, edited by Christopher Lloyd, Navy Records Society, Vol. IV (1952), p. 79.
[2] *Hakluytus Posthumus or Purchas His Pilgrimes*, Vol. XX (1907), p. 33.

There is general stir. "What noise?"

> The town is empty; on the brow o' the sea
> Stand ranks of people, and they cry "A sail!"   2.1.53

This scene of welcome has some likenesses to the farewell of Hawkins when he set out from Plymouth in June 1593 on his perilous South Sea voyage.

> "I looft near the shore, to give my farewell to all the inhabitants of the towne, whereof the most part were gathered together upon the Howe, to shew their gratefull correspondency, to the love and zeale, which I, my father, and predecessors, have ever borne to that place, as to our naturall and mother towne. And first with my noyse of trumpets, after with my waytes, and then with my other musicke, and lastly, with the artillery of my shippes, I made the best signification I could of a kinde farewell. This they answered with the waytes of the towne, and the ordinance on the shore, and with shouting of voyces; which with the fayre evening and silence of the night, were heard a great distance off."[1]

The firing of salutes is heard from the ship:

> They do discharge their shot of courtesy:
> Our friends at least.   2.1.56

This is strictly according to naval custom, the orders for salutes between ships and forts being "that they courteously salute one another with some guns and that the comer in begin first".[2] The same is observed as Othello's ship comes in:

> They give their greeting to the citadel:
> This likewise is a friend,   2.1.94

thus fulfilling a further purpose of the orders: "that so a convenient and timely notice may be taken one of another, and all practices, suspicions, and mistakes prevented and avoided".[3]

More ceremony follows. Marks of respect in keeping with Othello's rank as General are shown by the sounding of a trumpet as he goes ashore. Arrangements are made for official visits, "Come let us to the castle". Care is taken not to omit the traditional civilities to the master of the ship:

> Bring thou the master to the citadel;
> He is a good one,[4]   2.1.210

[1] *The Hawkins' Voyages*, edited by C. R. Markham, Hakluyt Society (1878), No. LVII, p. 112.
[2] *Boteler's Dialogues*, edited by W. G. Perrin, Navy Records Society (1929), p. 273.
[3] Boteler, p. 268.   [4] See Master, p. 57.

There are further routine orders: "Go to the bay, and disembark my coffers:" And lastly, a public celebration is proclaimed and shore leave granted from five o'clock till eleven.

> "every man put himself into triumph; some to dance, some to make bonfires, each man to what sport and revels his addiction leads him: . . . All offices are open, and there is full liberty of feasting from this present hour of five till the bell have told eleven." 2.2.4

It was an age of brilliant naval strategy, and in this action against the enemy, three points insisted on by Drake have been observed: to learn the design of an enemy; to keep intelligence from the enemy; to work for the advantage of wind and weather. The council took care of the first two, the command at sea of the last.

These sea scenes with their wholesome excitements and ex-hilaration introduce a heroic, valiant, practical world where the best qualities of men are brought out. They stand in the sharpest contrast to the dark imaginings, the intrigues and the horrors that are to follow. After this, the sea goes out and does not come in again except briefly at two culminating moments. In his fatal fixity of purpose, Othello is:

> Like to the Pontic sea,
> Whose icy current and compulsive course
> Ne'er feels retiring ebb, but keeps due on
> To the Propontic and the Hellespont; 3.3.454

And, when all is over, his thoughts turn once more to the sea:

> Here is my journey's end, here is my butt
> And very sea mark of my utmost sail. 5.2.266

The sea and its associations are a means of deepening the irony of events and the tragedy. The cool deliberations of the naval council, scrutinising the evidence and guarding against rash conclusions, are in significant contrast to the readiness to believe the worst and the blind credulousness that set convulsive passions to work as the drama unfolds. In the same way, when Cassio says:

> Tempests themselves, high seas, and howling winds,
> The gutter'd rocks, and congregated sands,
> Traitors ensteep'd to clog the guiltless keel,
> As having sense of beauty, do omit
> Their mortal natures, letting go safely by
> The divine Desdemona. 2.1.68

it adds to the darkness of Iago's treachery.

Othello, speaking in exultant sea imagery of his reunion with

Desdemona, is likewise blind to what is vulnerable in his own nature:

> If after every tempest come such calms,
> May the winds blow till they have waken'd death!
> And let the labouring bark climb hills of seas
> Olympus high, and duck again as low
> As hell's from heaven! 2.1.186

SEA DEFEAT

Antony and Cleopatra

Maritime supremacy was the great issue of Shakespeare's day, and the swaying fortunes of war led to much discussion of strategy and the causes of success or failure. Shakespeare is aware of laws and principles at work in all history, irrespective of age or epoch, and he condenses Plutarch's narrative of a long-drawn-out and fluctuating campaign in a way that brings these out.

The struggle at sea between Caesar Augustus and Antony is reduced to a study of two phases of a defeat. The first is an action broken off halfway through because of a disastrous divided command, the second is not an engagement at all, but a surrender. The scenes depicting these might have been made full of sensation, commotion and tumult because they lend themselves to that, but instead, problems of leadership and of strategy and a philosophy of history run through them. Shakespeare adapts his source to give emphasis to these, omitting incidents that would obscure them, and using the comments of minor characters to stress what has led to the outcome.

Antony's strategy and leadership are bad. Where they fall short is made clear in the drama itself, but this gains force if some principles on which Drake insisted are considered also. Reasoning against those who were offering very different advice, Drake wrote to the Queen on 13 April 1588:

> "Most gracious Sovereign:—I have received from Mr. Secretary some particular notes, and withal a commandment to answer them unto your Majesty."

Then comes his leading principle: "The advantage of time and place in all martial actions is half a victory; which being lost is irrecoverable."[1] Nelson, over two centuries later, was to go

---

[1] *State Papers Relating to the Defeat of the Spanish Armada Anno 1588*, edited by John L. Laughton, Navy Records Society, 2 vols. (1894), I, 147–48.

further: "Time is everything; five minutes makes the difference between a victory and a defeat."[1]

From this followed, in Drake's strategy, the importance of taking the offensive and striking the first blow, of forcing the enemy to fight at a disadvantage, of keeping designs secret and of surprise.

Now, in all these Antony fails and Caesar takes the right course. Caesar gains "the advantage of time and place".

> Is it not strange, Canidius
> That from Tarentum and Brundusium
> He could so quickly cut the Ionian sea,
> And take it Toryne? 3.7.20

> This speed of Caesar's carries beyond belief. 3.7.73

Cleopatra's nimble rejoinder points the lesson:

> Celerity is never more admired
> Than by the negligent.

Antony's intelligence service is poor, for Caesar's

> "power went out in such distractions as Beguiled all spies". 3.7 77

Caesar takes the initiative, and Antony allows him to keep it. He throws away his best chance of success which lies in fighting by land, for no better reason than that Caesar has dared him to fight at sea. He thus fights on the enemy's terms and has no conviction that one line of action is sounder than another. His veterans argue in vain that they

> Have used to conquer, standing on the earth,
> And fighting foot to foot. 3.7.65

He takes the irresponsible view:

> But if we fail
> We then can do't at land. 3.7.52

and gives himself up "merely to chance and hazard".

The Privy Council with whom Howard and Drake had a long struggle would have brought about a state of affairs much like this. The repeated "may be", "perchance", "might be" of their memoranda give the impression that they were content to fall back on methods of trial and error, and it is fortunate that the belief of both admirals in their own strategy was unshakeable.

The position of Antony is made worse by the fatal weakness of a divided command.

---

[1] *The Dispatches and Letters of Vice Admiral Lord Viscount Nelson*, edited by Nicholas H. Nicolas Vol. IV, p. 290.

Cleopatra says imperiously:

> A charge we bear i' the war,
> And, as the president of my kingdom, will
> Appear there for a man.   3.7.16

Whim takes the place of strategy as she decrees: "By sea! what else?" (28). The dismay of the officers: "our leader's led, And we are women's men," (69) foreshadows what happens. Cleopatra flees while the battle is yet undecided and Antony, "Leaving the fight in height, flies after her" (3.10.20). Comment, if it be needed, may best be restricted to the words of an official ruling:

> "For it is not the part of a General upon any occasion to leave his fleet, though for a time he may leave his ship."[1]

Disputes arising from joint command in enterprises against Spain were frequent between Admirals and Generals in the 1580's and 1590's. There had been some feeling between Howard and Essex in the expedition to Cadiz in 1596 and "there arose a great question—who should have the honour of the first going in".[2] Here in ancient history was an example, overwhelming and grotesque, of what twofold command could lead to if not based on strictly naval or military considerations.

To stress that it was bad strategy and bad leadership and not mischance that caused Antony's overthrow, Shakespeare omits, as inessential, Plutarch's mention of a successful move by Antony and also of a storm that delayed the battle.

He further works out a contrast in leadership that is original. Caesar is cool and collected. Antony

> Is valiant, and dejected; and, by starts
> His fretted fortunes give him hope, and fear
> Of what he has, and has not.   4.12.6

Antony is given to the waywardness, obstinacy, recklessness, excitableness and impetuousness so conspicuous in the conduct of Essex in the Islands Voyage of 1597 and also later. When balked, Antony takes refuge in the kind of foolhardy defiance that marks the outbursts of Essex: "though we eat ropes' ends and drink nothing but rain water, we will out".[3] So with Antony:

> I would they'ld fight i' th' fire or i' th' air;
> We'ld fight there too.   4.10.3

Antony is either silent when he should give orders or he explains

---

[1] Monson, Vol. III, p. 85.   [2] Monson, Vol. I, p. 347.
[3] Monson, Vol. II, p. 78. See p. 31.

too much. He is capricious and his officers do not know where they stand. Instead of encouraging his followers after a reverse, he says "I have lost my way for ever", 3.11.4. When they rally round him to make a fresh attempt, he indulges his own feelings without considering theirs:

> Tend me tonight;
> May be it is the period of your duty:
> Haply, you shall not see me more; or if,
> A mangled shadow. Perchance tomorrow
> You'll serve another master. I look on you
> As one that takes his leave. 4.2.24

When they are upset by this, he protests. "You take me in too dolorous a sense." Fleeting success throws him into an ecstasy, setbacks leave him crushed.

There is no discussion or questioning of plans in Caesar's camp; obedience is the law. Caesar has complete command, his orders are brief and final:

> *Caesar.* Taurus!
> *Taurus.* My lord?
> *Caesar.* Strike not by land: keep whole: provoke not battle
>   Till we have done at sea. Do not exceed
>   The prescript of this scroll: our fortune lies
>   Upon this jump. (*Exeunt*) 3.8.1

The leadership of Caesar Augustus is ennobled, for it is inspired by a vision before which mere personal triumph grows dim.

> The time of universal peace is near.
> Prove this a prosperous day, the three-nooked world
> Shall bear the olive freely. 4.6.6

Antony makes a bid to retrieve the first disaster but his second and, as it proves, last attempt shows that he has not learned anything from the earlier reverse. The initiative is again left to the enemy. Antony's aim should be to take them unawares or to outwit them, instead, he falls in with their plans:

> Their preparation is today by sea,
> We please them not by land. 4.10.1

The result is disaster. His ships go over to the other side without even a show of offering fight:

> All is lost!
> My fleet hath yielded to the foe; 4.12.9

Then follows the spectacle of a navy that has become demoralised, of men no longer conscious of fighting in a cause, indifferent to winning or losing, eager only to be out of danger and to be left to themselves:

> Yonder
> They cast their caps up and carouse together
> Like friends long lost. 4.12.11

Plutarch presents it as a friendly arrangement, Shakespeare brings out the ignominy.

In setting out this struggle at sea, Shakespeare avoids antiquarianism. Plutarch's references to galleys with three to ten banks of oars and his details of the build and management of Roman and Egyptian ships are omitted. The ships are fighting ships as Elizabethans and Jacobeans would, in a general way, think of them. Nor does he overlook the interest that comes from seeing history repeating itself:

> Your ships are not well manned
> Your mariners are muleters, reapers, people
> Ingrossed by swift impress; in Caesar's fleet
> Are those that often have 'gainst Pompey fought.
> Their ships are yare, yours heavy. 3.7.34

These advantages and disadvantages that Antony's advisers urge him to weigh up, are similar to those of the English and Spanish fleets which had been noted by Sir Thomas Fenner in his *Considerations*, written on 14 July, 1588:

"So mighty an army of three years' preparation, ... being gathered ... out of so many and so far countries, wherein there are in number above twenty thousand that have not tasted the seas before.... Withal their mariners, being of sundry nations, and by all the advertisements we can gather very unwilling to meet with our forces at sea, have been, since their first proceedings, by severe punishment and political orders kept together, otherwise their minds have been to run away."[1]

Unlike the uncertain sea terms in the English translation of Plutarch by North, Shakespeare's are accurate and precise, and there are more of them, because they are not confined to the sea scenes but are carried into the imagery throughout.

[1] *Defeat of the Spanish Armada*, Vol. I, pp. 240–41.

CEREMONIAL VISITS AT SEA

ABOARD POMPEY'S VESSEL

Antony and Cleopatra, Act II, scene 7

Plutarch tells how Pompey cast anchors into the sea to make his galley fast and built a bridge of wood to convey his guests to it, "and there he made them great cheer".

From no more than this, Shakespeare creates an original scene. He disregards the mention of a bridge or breakwater from ship to shore, preferring to make the guests come and go by barge with the naval ceremony of his own day. This enables him to make fuller use of colourful spectacle and musical instruments.

"For our ships of war being once afloat and predy, it is to be expected that some good company will come aboard; and it is fit to know how to entertain them with due and decent compliments and ceremonies."[1]

Shakespeare shows this being done. Serving men come on first, carrying a banquet and making shrewd comments on what it is "to have a name in great men's fellowship". Then, when Caesar, Antony, Lepidus, Pompey and others appear, a sennet, or set of four trumpets of different pitch, is sounded in accordance with the rules for the entertaining of a prince or admiral:

And being ready for his meat, the trumpets are to sound at the carrying of it up, and the music to be at hand to play when he is at it.[2]

The banquet scene is remarkable in its lifelikeness. Conviviality, pledging, eddying conversation, the melodrama of a whispered plot, revel, humour, treachery, song "Cup us, till the world go round", and music are all mingled. And dramatically, this has a direct bearing on later events. For here, in their unguarded moments, those who are competing for the sovereignty of the world reveal qualities that show how it was lost and won.

[1] Boteler, p. 264.　　　　　[2] Boteler, p. 266.

Menas, who in Plutarch is a pirate, is recast completely by Shakespeare. He is Pompey's trusted officer and is on the same footing as Antony's officer, Enobarbus, and they are fast friends. He is carrying out what today would be the duties of an Officer of the Watch who is responsible for the safety of the ship and must report any urgent matter to the captain at once. That is why he is able, without breach of courtesy, to have a private word with Pompey during the banquet. It is done with a formality of approach and withdrawal that makes it in order and takes away suspicion.

Menas is also responsible for the ship's routine, for the running of boats ashore, and for ceremony as well. He takes charge of an important part of this when the guests leave. A distinguished guest was "in the like manner to be waited upon at his departure, as he was at his coming in".[1] Shakespeare, to avoid repeating similar ceremonial compliments, prefers to omit the arrival and show the departure only.

Menas has tried to ensure that everything will go well. The barge has been lying alongside to take the guests ashore. The "squadron of the watch" has been standing by. It includes the trumpeters and musicians who are to sound a "loath-to-depart"[2] as the barge leaves the ship.

The banquet drags on. The revellers at last make their long expected, but, as it seems, sudden appearance. They go over the side. There are delays on the ship's ladder, cries of "Come down into the boat", and, as they help one another, "Take heed you fall not". The squadron of the watch has had a long wait, the men are overwatched, their keenness has gone. Menas recalls them sharply to their duty. "These drums, these trumpets, flutes! What!" Then, combining encouragement with command: "Let Neptune hear we bid a loud farewell To these great fellows." The "loath-to-depart" should ring out, but some are showing slackness; an important point of ceremony is about to go wrong. It is too much for the patience of a tired and tried Officer of the Watch, and he shouts at them: "Sound and be hanged—sound out!"[3] and then, when it is over, gives a gasp of relief: "Hoo!" and throws his cap in the air. The scene may have closed with ordnance going off in salute.

[1] Boteler, p. 266.
[2] The music has survived. See *The Mariner's Mirror*, Vol. IX (1923), p. 9.
[3] Today the order is "sound off".

"And being returned into his barge, after the trumpets have sounded a loath-to-depart, and that the barge is fallen off a fit and fair berth and distance from the ship, he is to have his farewell given him with so many guns as the ship is able to give; provided that they be always of an odd number."[1]

The sense of a state occasion and of being in a great ship is preserved throughout, even in the revelry, and this is achieved largely through the skilful use of naval ceremony.

PERICLES

The story makes it necessary for the Governor of Mytilene to see Pericles and the scene might well open with an interview taking place on board Pericles's ship. But Shakespeare chooses to lead up to the meeting with the ceremony that belongs to an official visit. In this, he draws on his knowledge of the uses of flags and ensigns and of the laws on the right of entry into harbours by foreign vessels.

It is a typical harbour scene. The ship is lying at anchor in view of the shore, "from the deck you may discern the place". Barges and boats are coming and going, and arrangements are being made for taking provisions on board:

> let us beseech you
> That for our gold we may provision have,
> Wherein we are not destitute for want,
> But weary for the staleness. 5.1.53

There were many incidents of this kind in Drake's voyages.

The governor has noted the entry of this foreign ship, "Lysimachus our Tyrian ship espies", and also its "banners sable, trimm'd with rich expense;" and he puts out in his barge (5, Chorus 18).

Colours and ensigns "are placed in the sterns or poops of ships; and few ships there are, whether men-of-war or merchant men that are without them. And their service is, that when any strange ships meet one with another at sea, or find one another in any harbour or road, by the showing abroad these Ensigns or Colours, it is known one to another of what country they are, and to what place they belong."[2]

---

[1] Boteler, pp. 266–67. Anachronism is not a relevant charge.　　　[2] Boteler, p. 274.

Nor is this all:

> "But besides this use, in great ships, and especially such as belong to the King, they are often used by way of trim and bravery; and are then hung out at every yard arm, and at the heads of the masts."[1]

Pericles's vessel is a "great ship", belonging to a king, and is dressed in this way.

The Governor's barge comes alongside and a sailor reports to Helicanus, the deputy of Pericles:

> Sir, there is a barge put off from Mytilene,
> And in it is Lysimachus the governor,
> Who craves to come aboard. What is your will? 5.1.3

The reply is: "That he have his." But Helicanus sees that no point of ceremony is omitted: "Call up some gentlemen." And he instructs them: "Gentlemen, there is some of worth would come aboard: I pray, greet him fairly." The gentlemen, with the sailors, go down the ship's ladder into the waiting barge and then escort the Governor on board their own ship (5.1.1–12). Formal compliments are exchanged and the reason for the visit stated:

> Seeing this goodly vessel ride before us,
> I made to it to know of whence you are. 5.1.18

This, again, is according to rule and custom.

> "In brief, no stranger of what condition soever ought to open his flag in any port of England, or in any place within any of his Majesty's dominions where there is any ship of his Majesty's own or in his service, upon the penalty (at the least, and that upon submission) of losing her flag, and to pay for the expense in powder that shall be spent in compelling there unto."[2]

Before answering, Helicanus makes sure who the visitor is. "First, what is your place?", and on being told, with formal precision, "I am the governor of this place you lie before," he in turn states, "Sir, Our vessel is of Tyre, in it the king;" and conducts the Governor to the king's pavilion (5.1.20–23).

All is done as English naval custom required. Ceremony and compliment give ease and grace where otherwise official scrutiny of this sort might create suspicion or a sense of being challenged.

---

[1] Boteler, p. 275.   [2] Boteler, pp. 271–72.

ADDITIONAL CEREMONY

Topsails were lowered or struck as a mark of respect or sign of
submission. This ceremony is referred to figuratively several
times. Warwick scorns to "bear so low a sail to strike" to Glouces-
ter, but Margaret "Must strike her sail and learn awhile to serve".
When Prince Hal succeeds to the throne, the Lord Chief Justice
fears that "all will be overturned", and Warwick, also, believes
that many nobles will find that they "must strike sail to spirits of
vile sort".[1]

Enobarbus makes adroit use of the figure. When Antony asks
him, "Woo't thou fight well?", his reply is, "I'll strike and cry
Take all!" Antony takes it to mean that he will set upon the foe
with all he can deliver and is satisfied—"Well said".[2] But
Enobarbus is speaking in a double sense. In his asides, he has
already made plain that he cannot follow Antony's fortunes any
longer:

> I will seek Some way to leave him 3.13.201

and earlier, with thoughts turning to the sea and ships, he had
reasoned with himself:

> thou art so leaky
> That we must leave thee to thy sinking.   3.13.63

His veiled answer continues the nautical metaphor and means
that he will lower sail and capitulate for, as a leader, Antony has
failed him.

Salutes at sea were also exchanged by lowering flags or ensigns.

"It is requirable that all ships and fleets, being inferiors
either in respect of sovereignty, or place, or part, or any the
like relations, do express an acknowledgment and submission
by the taking in of their own flags, whensoever they meet with
any others that are justly their superiors in any of these
respects."[3]

It was a proud and stately spectacle:

> argosies with portly sail,
> Like signiors and rich burghers of the flood,
> Or as it were the pageants of the sea,
> Do overpeer the petty traffickers,
> That curtsy to them, do them reverence,
> As they fly by them with their woven wings.   M. of V. 1.1.

[1] 3 *Hen. VI* 5.1.52; 3 *Hen. VI* 3.3.5; 2 *Hen. IV* 5.2.18.
[2] *Ant. and Cleo.* 4.2.6 ff.   [3] Boteler, p. 271.

Saluting with guns was more frequent. On some occasions, as in *Othello*, it was essential, but much of it came to be looked upon as an abuse. Monson deplored "the lavish use of shooting for pleasure at the meeting of ships, passing by castles, and banqueting aboard", and he maintained "there is more powder wastefully spent in this sort than against an enemy".[1]

Hamlet's description of the revels and feasting at Elsinore is not unlike what happened during a banquet on board:

> No jocund health that Denmark drinks today,
> But the great cannon to the clouds shall tell,
> And the king's rouse the heaven shall bruit again,
> Respeaking earthly thunder,   1.2.125

Celebrations of this kind actually took place when the English ambassador received the King of Denmark on board the *Golden Lion* at Elsinore in July 1603:

> "That afternoone the king went aboard the English ship, and had a banket prepared for him upon the upper decks, which were hung with an Awning of cloathe of Tissue: every health reported sixe, eight or ten shot of great Ordinance, so that during the king's abode, the ship discharged 160 shot."[2]

This was repeated on a grand scale when the King of Denmark paid a state visit to England in 1614. King James and his Queen were entertained on board the Danish flagship off Gravesend, and:

> "At every health, there were from the ships of Denmark and the forts some three or fourscore great shot discharged, and of these thundering volleys there were between forty and fifty. You would have thought that Jupiter had been invited."[3]

[1] Monson, Vol. II, p. 243
[2] *The Annales of England*, by John Stow (1605), 4to, p. 1436.
[3] *The Court of King James the First*; by Dr. Godfrey Goodman, 2 vols. (1839), II, p. 140.

SEA BURIAL

When told of the death of his queen at the height of the storm, Pericles exclaims in grief:

> you gods!
> Why do you make us love your goodly gifts,
> And snatch then straight away? We here below
> Recall not what we give, and therein may
> Vie honour with you. 3.1.23

But his lament is cut short by the sailors in seaphrase that recalls stern reality and the urgency of the hour:

> "Sir, your queen must *overboard*; the sea
> *works high*, the wind is loud, and will not *lie*
> till the ship be *cleared* of the dead." 3.1.46 ff.

Pericles remonstrates, "That's your superstition":

> "Pardon us, sir; with us at sea it hath been
> still observed, and we are strong in custom.
> Therefore briefly yield her, for she must overboard
> straight!"

He must accept for there is no other way, "As you think meet— most wretched queen!", and he continues his lament in words meant to lead up to a ritual prayer:

> th' unfriendly elements
> Forgot thee utterly: nor have I time
> To give thee hallowed to thy grave, but straight
> Must cast thee, scarcely coffined, in the ooze;
> Where, for a monument upon thy bones,
> And aye-remaining lamps, the belching whale
> And humming water must o'erwhelm thy corpse,
> Lying with simple shells. 3.1.57 ff.

Then come some final directions:

> O Lychorida,
> Bid Nestor bring me spices, ink and paper,
> My casket and my jewels; and bid Nicander
> Bring me the satin coffer.
> Hie thee, whiles I say
> A priestly farewell to her.

The sailors report that all is in order and a chest "caulked and bitumed" in readiness. Pericles's disciplined acknowledgement follows:

I thank thee . . .
> Go thy ways, good mariner;
> I'll bring the body presently.

The committal to the deep is not shown. It was the custom "to
ring the knell and farewell with some guns the which . . . are
always to be of an even number".[1] and it may have been intended
that the scene should end in this way.

[1] Boteler, p. 268. See p. 121 (Pistol).

SUCCOUR SHIPS

Carrying supplies and bringing help and succour has always been part of the navy's duty and there were many calls in Elizabethan times. Early in *Pericles*, a scene is partly based on this particular side of naval work. To a famine-stricken city which is reduced to extreme misery, comes news that "A portly sail of ships make hitherward", but instead of raising hope, it increases despair:

> some neighbouring nation,
> Taking advantage of our misery
> Hath stuffed the hollow vessels with their power,
> To beat us down, the which are down already.   1.4.60 ff.

Even when it is urged that,

> by the semblance
> Of their white flags displayed, they bring us peace
> And come to us as favourers, not as foes,

this is met with, "Who makes the fairest show means most deceit."

But it proves to be a genuine expedition for the relief of distress, and it is conducted with proper regard for regulations and ceremony. A white flag was a regular signal even in privateering voyages. It showed that a ship had no hostile intention, but had come to trade or bring succour or that it sought the shelter of an anchorage.

> "Presently the English canoe ran up a white flag in what seemed to be a signal of peace, and by the governor's order another such flag was shown on land and a boat came ashore from the English pinnace and canoe. On behalf of the governor a demand was made to know what they wanted."[1]

Something similar happens here. The governor of the city gives instructions in an official manner:

> Go tell their general we attend him here,
> To know for what he comes, and whence he comes,
> And what he craves.

[1] *English Privateering Voyages . . . 1588–1595*, edited by Kenneth R. Andrews, Hakluyt Society (1959), pp. 161–62.

Pericles, on coming ashore, reassures them all:

> Let not our ships and number of our men
> Be like a beacon fired t'amaze your eyes,

and makes the purpose of his visit plain: "these our ships . . .
Are stored with corn to make your needy bread."

He ends by asking "harbourage for ourself, our ships and men",
as Drake and other voyagers so often did.

MOBILISATIONS

Why this same strict and most observant watch——
And why such daily cast of brazen cannon——
Why such impress of shipwrights, whose sore task
Does not divide the Sunday from the week,   *Hamlet* 1.1.75

Hopes of avenging the defeat of the Armada in 1588 had never died down in Spain and preparations for further attempts against England were renewed year after year. The threat of invasion caused great alarm in 1590 and orders were issued to register for service all seamen, fishermen and gunners between sixteen and sixty years of age and to concentrate ships in readiness at Portsmouth. Again in 1594, there were musters and plans for meeting attack. To play upon fears of invasion was one way of delaying or preventing English expeditions to the West Indies and other Spanish possessions. "The Spaniards most subtly let slip no opportunity to put us into an amazement, thereby to dissolve or divert the expedition, and sent four galleys from Blavet in Brittany to seize some part of our coast, that so we might apprehend a greater force was to follow. These galleys landed at Penzance in Cornwall, where, finding the town abandoned, they sacked and burnt it: but this design of theirs took little effect, for the voyage proceeded nevertheless."[1]

On the principle that it is better to attack than to be attacked, the Cadiz voyage of 1596 was undertaken by Howard and Essex "against such mighty forces as now are advertised from all parts of Christendom, to be already prepared by the King of Spain, and which are to be mightily increased, to invade her Majesty's realm, as was attempted in 1588".[2]

In the following year, a Spanish fleet appeared in sight of England with the usual unsettling effect.

But most sensational of all was the great mobilisation of 1599 so clearly recalled in *Hamlet*. News came that a Spanish Armada had asked for permission to put into Brest. Panic reigned in London. There were feverish preparations for defence both by land and sea. The city and the Thames were placed under the

[1] Monson, Vol. I, pp. 312–13.   [2] Monson, Vol. I, p. 376 and note.

special command of the Earl of Cumberland who "got together all the lighters, boats, western barges, cables and anchors that were to be found," to make a defensive bridge, "giving out that with 1,500 musketeers he would defend that bridge or lose his life upon it (but God forbid he should have been put to it)". Frenzy mounted and was acute for two days. "Upon Monday, towards evening, came news (yet false), that the Spaniards were landed in the Isle of Wight, which bred such a fear and consternation in this town as I would little have looked for."[1]

The danger passed, but not in a way that contrasted too sharply with what had gone before, or that made the alerts, alarms and frantic preparations seem overdone, for the speed and enterprise shown "in drawing together so great an army by land, and rigging her royal navy to sea, in so little a space of time was so admired in other countries that they received a terror by it; and many that came from beyond sea said, 'The Queen was never more dreaded for anything she ever did' ".[2]

> ... and this, I take it,
> Is the main motive of our preparations,
> The source of this our watch, and the chief head
> Of this post-haste and romage in the land. 1.1.104

[1] Chamberlain to Carleton, Monson, Vol. II, p. 104.
[2] Monson, Vol. II, p. 86.

A ROYAL FLEET PUTS TO SEA

The history plays with their expeditions and invasions enable Shakespeare to bring in various naval events and incidents and, in so doing, he may add to his historical sources.

A vivid, animated and original picture of a fleet putting to sea is given in *Henry V.* Historically, it is justified because that monarch built up a great navy, but Shakespeare's "fleet majestical" has the heroic splendour of one of his own day, and is described in the spirit of Howard:

"My good Lord, there is here the gallantest company of captains, soldiers, and mariners that I think ever was seen in England."[1]

> Suppose that you have seen
> The well-appointed king at Hampton pier
> Embark his royalty; and his brave fleet
> With silken streamers the young Phoebus fanning:
> Play up your fancies, and in them behold
> Upon the hempen tackle ship-boys climbing;
> Hear the shrill whistle which doth order give
> To sounds confus'd; behold the threaden sails,
> Borne with th' invisible and creeping wind,
> Draw the huge bottoms through the furrow'd sea,
> Breasting the lofty surge. O, do but think
> You stand upon the rivage and behold
> A city on th' inconstant billows dancing;
> For so appears this fleet majestical,
> Holding due course to Harfleur. Follow, follow!
> Grapple your minds to sternage of this navy,
> And leave your England, as dead midnight still   3 *Chorus* 3 ff.

There is a companion picture of the return in triumph:

> Now bear we the king
> Toward Calais: grant him there; there seen,
> Heave him away upon your winged thoughts
> Athwart the sea. Behold, the English beach
> Pales in the flood with men, with wives, and boys,
> Whose shouts and claps out-voice the deep-mouth'd sea,
> Which, like a mighty whiffler, 'fore the king
> Seems to prepare his way: so let him land.   5 *Chorus* 5 ff.

---

[1] *Defeat of the Spanish Armada*, Vol. I, p. 190 (Howard to Burghley, 28 May 1588).

To complete the scene, Shakespeare "by a lower but by loving likelihood", ventures a comparison with the hoped-for return of Essex:

> Were now the general of our gracious empress,
> As in good time he may, from Ireland coming,
> Bringing rebellion broached on his sword,
> How many would the peaceful city quit
> To welcome him! much more, and much more cause,
> Did they this Harry. 5 *Chorus* 30 ff.

All terms belonging to seamanship and navigation are, as usual, exact, so, too, is the knowledge shown of the organisation and working of warships.

PUTTING TO SEA

Throughout the plays, there is much putting to sea. In all but a few some character takes ship or has been a voyager. Little may be made of it, a remark, a mere mention, a brief word of farewell, and no more. The circumstances are as various as the characters themselves and the scenes and incidents and feelings are such as will recur as long as men go to sea.

Leavetaking and embarking come into the early part of *Two Gentlemen of Verona*. An anxious parent waits by the quay side:

> my father at the road
> Expects my coming, there to see me shipped.   1.1.53

Youthful friends have their sentimental farewell interrupted by an incorrigible servant who runs up with luggage, breathless and only just in time. The tearful parting of the lovers, Proteus and Julia, is made more uneasy by reminders of time and tide and the call "Sir Proteus, you are stayed for" (2.2.19). Later, another tardy servant sets everyone on edge, "you'll lose the tide if you tarry any longer", or at cross purposes, "Come, come away, man; I was sent to call thee. . . . Wilt thou go?" (2.3.54).

In *Hamlet*, there is a parting scene with words of advice from brother to sister:

> My necessaries are embarked, farewell,   1.3.1
>
> Farewell, Ophelia, and remember well
> What I have said to you,   1.3.84

and also from father to son:

> Yet here Laertes? aboard, aboard for shame!
> The wind sits in the shoulder of your sail,
> And you are stayed for. There—my blessing
>   with thee,   1.3.55 ff.

then, detaining him further,

> And these few precepts in thy memory
> Look thou character.

It is a pleasant scene of family affection and it deepens the tragedy that follows.

Embarking of a different sort comes later. The crafty King has

all in readiness to ship Hamlet to "especial safety". "The bark
is ready and the wind at help", and the atmosphere becomes
sinister as he urges his minions:

> tempt him with speed aboard,
> Delay it not, I'll have him hence tonight.
> Away! for everything is sealed and done.   4.3.54

The most romantic putting to sea comes in *The Winter's Tale*.
Florizel and Perdita, when they cannot win the king's consent to
their union, decide on a "wild dedication" of themselves "to
unpathed waters, undreamed shores". All practical matters,
navigation, provisions, whither bound, are swept aside. The sea is
to take charge:

> I have
> A vessel rides fast by, but not prepared
> For this design.   4.4.501

When asked, "Have you thought on A place whereto you'll go?",
Florizel's answer is "Not any yet", and only with difficulty are
they persuaded to "a course more promising". 4.4.537ff.

The last sight of shore is a theme that tends to be poignant, and
Shakespeare touches on it briefly in some early lines:

> as one on shore
> Gazing upon a late embarked friend,
> Till the wild waves will have him seen no more,   *Ven. and Adon.* 817

These have a wider interest because of the contrast they offer to
the mature art with which the same kind of scene is treated in
Cymbeline. The exile strains his eyes as the ship makes from shore,
gathering way as land, and the watcher there, are lost to view:

> for so long
> As he could make me with this eye, or ear,
> Distinguish him from others, he did keep
> The deck, with glove or hat or handkerchief,
> Still waving, as the fits and stirs of's mind
> Could best express how slow his soul sailed on,
> How swift his ship.   1.4.8

The effect of objects growing less, melting from "the smallness
of a gnat to air" is linked with the forlorn feelings that well up in
one left behind:

> I would have broke mine eye strings, cracked them but
> To look upon him, till the diminution
> Of space had pointed him sharp as my needle:
> Nay, followed him, till he had melted from
> The smallness of a gnat to air: and then
> Have turned mine eye and wept.   1.4.17

D

The detail of glove, hat, handkerchief is used to add naturalness. All is moving and human, but the emotion though deep is kept restrained.

The feelings of one eager for the first view of a land where she is to be queen are voiced by Margaret in 2 *Henry VI*. Her impassioned, tense words show a struggle to put former attachments aside, and to convince all who hear that the new devotion is fervent.

> And even with this I lost fair England's view,
> And bid mine eyes be packing with my heart,
> And called them blind and dusky spectacles,
> For losing ken of Albion's wished coast.   3.2.109

STORMS

"In her Majesty's eighteen years' war with Spain by sea, her fleets were employed on the Spanish coast, in the Indies, and other places, continually abiding and enduring the fury of all winds and weather, never out of motion and working in troublesome water, never for the space of three, four, five, or six months so much as putting into harbour, or anchoring, or having any other refreshment from shore, but still tossing on the waves of mountainous seas."[1]

Never had so much been known and written about storm and tempest or the might and terror of the ocean.

The Cambridge mathematician, Edward Wright, who went to sea to test some of his theories and sailed with the Earl of Cumberland's expedition to the Azores in 1589, pauses in the course of his work, "Certain Errors in Navigation", 1599, to describe their stormy voyage.

"These storms were so terrible, that there were some in our company, who confessed they had gone to sea for the space of twenty years, and had never seen the like: and vowed that if ever they returned safe home, they would never come to sea again."[2]

The ship was so buffeted and storm-tossed that they feared it "would have shaken in sunder".

"Herewith, our mainsail was torn from the yard, and blown overboard quite away into the sea without recovery: and our other sails so rent and torn, from side to side some of them, that hardly any of them escaped whole. The raging waves and foaming surges of the sea came rolling, like mountains one after another; and overraked the waist of the ship, like a mighty river running over it."[3]

[1] Monson, Vol. II, p. 263.
[2] *An English Garner Voyages and Travels,* edited by C. R. Beazley, Vol. II (1903), pp. 207–208.
[3] Ibid.

One of the "voluntary gentleman" in Essex's Islands Voyage of 1597, John Donne, later Dean of St. Paul's, declared in some heartfelt verses, "Compar'd with these stormes, death is but a qualm", and, after what he had endured himself, the plight of the prophet seemed even more hapless than he had thought it before:

Jonas, I pitty thee, and curse those men,
Who when the storm rag'd most, did wake thee then;[1]

Narratives of voyages, reports, despatches from sea, ship's logs, journals and letters added their own accounts, and much that was never set down at all would enliven the talk of those returning from sea as they told, and perhaps tried to enact, what they had been through.

To bring storm and tempest into drama, at a time when the freedom as well as the prosperity of the nation was bound up with what happened at sea and the nation's eyes were turned there, was understandable. But it was not an easy undertaking for one as exacting with himself as Shakespeare. Edward Wright's rule, "the groundes of Art . . . so much as is possible ought to be without all error", was one that he too held to be binding. He would not have been satisfied with giving an illusion of seafaring in the hope that what was seen and heard would be accepted as a faithful likeness of what would really take place. Other playwrights might bring on characters with names like Captain Seagull[2] using sea terms incidentally, or in a way that would not be heard at sea; but, in Shakespeare, all is kept unforced and true to life. Nor was he content, in his storm scenes, merely to repeat a set piece with variations. The scenes in *Othello*, *The Tempest*, *The Winter's Tale*, *Pericles*, are all different from one another, as are the brief storm passages that come into other plays.

THE TEMPEST

"A tempest, which they count a degree above a storm."[3]

Act I, scene I

The ship is a royal ship,[4] "the King's ship", "our royal good

---

[1] "The Storme."   [2] *Eastward Ho*, Act III, scene 3.   [3] Mainwaring, Vol. II, p. 242.
[4] The voyage of King George VI to South Africa in H.M.S. *Vanguard* is a parallel.

and gallant ship", part of a "royal fleet". This is never left in doubt, and it accounts for the discipline that is observed:

> "When sudden and fierce tempest befalls, our words of command are in brief for there is no time to be tedious."[1]

Orders are given in this way and the seamen carry them out in silence in the proper naval manner:

> "No man is to speak but the officers . . . so as . . . things may be done without noise or confusion."[2]

Fleet instructions insisted on this necessary form of discipline and are explicit:

> "If the master or his mate bid heave out the main topsail, the master's mate, boatswain's mate or quartermaster which hath charge of that sail shall with his company perform it, without calling out to others and without rumour."[2]

What would happen were it otherwise can be seen from the behaviour of the courtiers who come on deck and distract the mariners with their clamour. The Boatswain rebukes them: "You mar our labour." When they keep it up, just as he gives a further important order, he breaks out with, "A plague upon this howling! they are louder than the weather or our office". It is not until the mariners' efforts prove vain, and they have to give over, that a cry goes up from them: "All lost, to prayers, to prayers! all lost!"

The interruptions of the courtiers are well placed. They come between the orders, and thus appear to give time for one set to be carried out and to take effect, before the next set is given.

The manoeuvres described are difficult and some would be attempted only in an emergency. Quickness and resource are needed, and a degree of skill in seamanship that comes only with long experience. Everything likely to save the ship is tried. The island is near, a violent onshore wind is blowing. The ship must weather or sail past the island, or else be driven so far in that running aground will be inevitable: "fall to 't, yarely, or we run ourselves aground: bestir, bestir." All that is done is meant to prevent this. To check the drift to leeward, the order, "Take in the topsail", is given. The Boatswain knows that, above all else,

---

[1] Boteler, p. 162.   [2] *Fighting Instructions 1530–1816*, pp. 41–42.

they must have "sea room" or room to manoeuvre. If only they
have that, the storm can do its worst, and so he shouts at it,
"Blow till thou burst thy wind, if room enough!" But still the ship
makes towards the shore. The next order, "Down with the top
mast! yare! lower, lower!", is meant to ease the ship by reducing
weight aloft, make the vessel roll less, and check the continuing
drift shorewards.

Opinion was divided about striking topmasts, but there is a
good reason for doing so here.

> "And as for the striking of the topmasts in this extremity of
> tempest, I am of his mind (though many are to the contrary)
> who holdeth that a ship is the wholesomer in the sea (though it
> be in a storm or tempest) when her topmasts are up, than when
> they are struck, and that she hath better way through it; so
> that when there is sea room enough it is the safest course not to
> strike them."[1]

Here, however, they do not have "sea room enough" as the
Boatswain's concern shows, and striking the topmast is justifiable.

To keep the ship close to the wind and away from the shore,
until they can gain the open sea, is the aim of the next manoeuvre,
"Bring her to try with main-course". The main course is another
term for the mainsail.

> "Trying is to have no more sail forth but the mainsail, the
> tack aboard, the bowline set up, the sheet close aft, and the helm
> tied down close aboard."[2]

An important point in the manoeuvre is that, "A ship *a-try* with
her mainsail (unless it be an extraordinary grown sea) will make
her way two points afore the beam."[2] That is what they hope the
ship will do, but it does not happen. Instead of heading out to sea,
it continues to be blown towards the island. In the hope of being
able to keep clear of the leeshore, another order, "Lay her a-hold,
a-hold!" is given. This is the only known example of the term in
print, but it survives in New England, and is used there in handling
yachts and sailing craft. It means to bring a vessel close to the wind
so as to hold it or keep it.[3] To do so, more sail must be set and a
further order follows, "set her two courses;" that is, set the fore-

---

[1] Boteler, p. 162.   [2] Mainwaring, Vol. II, p. 250.
[3] The derivation of this term and its connection with "haul" are discussed in an article in
the *American Neptune*, V (July 1951), pp. 209-14.

sail in addition to the mainsail. The final directions, "off to sea again;" "lay her off", indicate what the result should be.

The ship is sound, the seamen are disciplined, the right orders are given. Some of the newer manoeuvres of the day, even one that was debatable, have been tried, but all without success. For Prospero is working his magic and they are controlled by his "potent art". They believe their ship has struck, "We split, we split, we split!", and do not realise that all is

> So safely ordered, that there is no soul
> No, not so much perdition as an hair
> Betid to any creature in the vessel.   1.2.29

Shakespeare could not have written a scene of this kind without taking great pains to grasp completely how a ship beset with these difficulties would have to be handled. He has not only worked out a series of manoeuvres, but has made exact use of the professional language of seamanship, knowing that if this were not strictly used aboard ship, the seamen would not know what they were required to do; and that, without it, the scene would not be realistic and lifelike.

He could not have come by this knowledge from books, for there were no works on seamanship in his day, nor were there any nautical word lists or glossaries, though several manuals had been published on navigation which, however, is a different art.[1]

The scene on board is followed by a further account of the storm itself when Prospero asks Ariel:

> Hast thou, spirit,
> Perform'd to point the tempest that I bade thee?

He makes his report, naming the different parts of a tall ship correctly,[2] and also telling how he had contrived to play the part of St. Elmo's fire, the "sea-fire" that was attracting much attention because of what was told of it by voyagers.

> I flam'd amazement: sometime I'd divide,
> And burn in many places; on the topmast,
> The yards and boresprit, would I flame distinctly,
> Then meet and join. Jove's lightnings, the precursors
> O' the dreadful thunderclaps, more momentary
> And sight outrunning were not.   1.2.198

This poetic description has details that are lacking in longer accounts in prose.

---

[1] See p. xii.   [2] See p. 105.

"Sir George Summers being upon watch, had an apparition of a little round light, like a faint Starre, trembling and streaming along with a sparkeling blaze, halfe the height upon the Maine Mast, and shooting sometimes from Shroud to Shroud, tempting to settle as it were upon any of the foure Shrouds: and for three or foure houres together, or rather more, halfe the night it kept with us; running sometimes along the Maine-yard to the very end, and then returning."[1]

But, picturesque as this is, there is nothing about that characteristic dividing and flaming "distinctly",[2] and then joining again, which Shakespeare makes the chief feature in his description.

STORMS IN *PERICLES*

In *Pericles*, the sea, ever-changing and unpredictable in its working, has the part of a principal character. Without it there would be no drama. Pericles soon comes to know what it is to be the victim of its seeming caprice and his words:

> A man whom both the waters and the wind,
> In that vast tennis court, hath made the ball
> For them to play upon,   2.1.59

have an echo of Drake's *Voyage About the World* with its "rowling seas, which tossed them, like a ball in a racket".[3] What is seen and heard of "the rough seas that spare not any man", "the seas Where's hourly trouble for a minute's ease", "the shipman's toil, With whom each minute threatens life or death",[4] leads up to one great storm scene which is the climax of the play.

The force and relentlessness of the storm are brought out in Pericles's beseeching words:

> The god of this great vast, rebuke these surges,
> Which wash both heaven and hell; and thou that hast
> Upon the winds command, bind them in brass,
> Having called them from the deep! O, still
> Thy deaf'ning dreadful thunders; gently quench
> Thy nimble sulphurous flashes!   3.1.1–6

[1] *Purchas His Pilgrimes*, Vol. XIX (1906), 11.
[2] In the sense of "in several places at the same time".
[3] *The World Encompassed By Sir Francis Drake*, edited by W. S. W. Vaux, Hakluyt Society (1854), p. 85.
[4] *Pericles* 2.1.130, 2.4.44, 1.3.23.

Entreaty gives place to anger against the raging wind:

> Thou stormest venomously;
> Wilt thou spit all thyself? The seaman's whistle
> Is as a whisper in the ears of death,
> Unheard.   3.1.7

Each phase of the storm is marked by a fateful happening on board, one born, one dead, one washed overboard. A sense of the fury of the tempest and the surging commotion is kept up by linking description with action. One passes into the other as the mariners battle and stake all on their efforts:

> Slack the bolins there!
> Blow, and split thyself.   3.1.43

There is desperate concern about sea room:

> But sea-room, and the brine and cloudy
> billow kiss the moon, I care not.   3.1.45

And even the hope of reaching harbour, which buoys them up and nerves them on, is tempered with:

> "if the wind cease".[1]   3.1.76

The scene does not have a connected series of manoeuvres like those in *The Tempest*. The difficulties of making the ship answer the helm and of altering course are not shown. But the storm lives in the memories of those who have suffered through it, and Marina later tells the tale as she has had it from others, using the sea wording and keeping the lifelikeness. This makes the earlier scene more complete by giving a picture of the leadership and fearlessness of Pericles, and by showing also his quickness and resource in rushing to the security of a hold on the mast as a great wave crashes on board and washes an unwary seaman from the yards. The mariners, too, are seen at their exhausting tasks, struggling against the elements, and caught in what seems to them threefold confusion as they bound from stem to stern, and strive to carry out the rapid series of orders from the Boatswain before the main mast and the Master abaft it:

> My father, as nurse says, did never fear,
> But cried "*Good seamen!*" to the sailors, galling
> His kingly hands, *haling ropes*;
> And, *clasping to the mast*, endured a *sea*
> That almost *burst the deck*.
> Never was *waves nor wind* more violent;
> And from the *ladder-tackle washes off*
> A *canvas-climber*. "Ha!" says one, "Wilt out?"

[1] See pp. 63–4.

> And with a dropping industry they *skip*
> From *stem to stern*; the *boatswain whistles*, and
> The *master* calls and trebles their confusion[1]   4.1.52 ff.

Pericles, "galling His kingly hands, haling ropes", is upholding
the tradition of Drake.

> "For I must have the gentleman to haul and draw with the
> mariner and the mariner with the gentleman. What! let us show
> ourselves all to be of a company and let us not give occasion
> to the enemy to rejoice at our decay and overthrow. I would
> know him, that would refuse to set his hand to a rope, but I
> know there is not any such here."[2]

SEA AND SKY

The poetic figure of the angry sea invading the sky is not
unusual in classical poetry, but Shakespeare need not be thought
of as influenced mainly by a literary fashion when he brings it in.
The idea itself is not so fanciful or extravagant as it might at first
appear, because sea and sky do seem to meet on the horizon line:

> Let's to the seaside, ho!
> As well to see the vessel that's come in
> As to throw out our eyes for brave Othello,
> Even till we make the Main and the aerial blue
> An indistinct regard.   *Oth.* 2.1.36

This becomes more pronounced in stormy weather with low
cloud and limited visibility. Indeed, in violent gales and tempests
all distinction between air and sea is lost. Spray rises in curtains,
"The chiding billow seems to pelt the clouds;" (*Oth.* 2.1.12), and
everything becomes enveloped in thick haze. What the onlooker
seems to see can be made very real by Shakespeare in everyday
speech without relying on poetic language at all.

> I have seen two such sights, by sea and by land!
> But I am not to say it is a sea, for it is now the sky:
> betwixt the firmament and it you cannot thrust a
> bodkin's point.   *W. Tale* 3.3.83

Heightened description was not left to dramatists and poets. It is
found in Strachey's *True Reportory of the Wracke*[3] and in the journals
of other voyagers:

---

[1] The nautical and technical wording is notable, See p. 149.
[2] *Drake and the Tudor Navy* by Julian S. Corbett, 2 vols., Vol. I (1898), p. 262.
[3] *Purchas His Pilgrimes*, Vol. XIX (1906), 7.

"The Sea swelled above the Clouds, and gave battell unto Heaven. It could not be said to raine, the waters like whole Rivers did flood in the ayre."[1]

In the same vein, Miranda speaks of the sea as "mounting to the Welkin's cheek" (*Temp.* 1.2.4), and Titus Andronicus finds it "threatening the welkin" (3.1.223). Even blunt Casca, becoming overwrought, can say:

> I have seen
> Th' ambitious ocean swell and rage and foam,
> To be exalted with the threat'ning clouds. *Julius Caesar* 1.3.6

Tempest and turbulence are not confined to storm scenes. They may illustrate ideas of upheaval and chaos, as in the speech of Ulysses on degree and basic order:

> Take but degree away. ——
> the bounded waters
> Should lift their bosoms higher than the shores,
> And make a sop of all this solid globe: *Troil. and Cress.* 1.3.111

The distraught and outraged Lear, calling for the dissolution all things:

> Bids the wind blow the earth into the sea,
> Or swell the curled waters 'bove the main,
> That things might change or cease. *K. Lear* 3.1.5

and Northumberland's grief and frustration find an outlet in similar words:

> now let not Nature's hand
> Keep the wild flood confined! let Order die! *2 Hen. IV* 1.1.153

SHIPWRECK

> Our hint of woe
> Is common; every day, some sailor's wife
> The masters of some merchant, and the merchant,
> Have just our theme of woe; but for the miracle,
> I mean our preservation, few in millions
> Can speak like us: then wisely, good sir, weigh
> Our sorrow with our comfort.   *Tempest* 2.1.3 ff.

Scenes or accounts of shipwreck begin in *The Comedy of Errors* and continue at intervals to the last plays. The account with which the earliest of the comedies opens has more incident than is found in the others, because all that happens is part of the framework of the story. With darkness and tempest, comes the first mischance:

> The sailors sought for safety by our boat,
> And left the ship, then sinking ripe, to us.   1.1.76

Lashed to a mast, the merchant, his wife, their sons and adopted charges float "obedient to the stream" until the mast is "encountered by a mighty rock" and "splitted in the midst". One half, "with lesser weight", is "carried with more speed before the wind", and the three still lashed to it are taken up by fishermen. The remaining three are rescued by another ship which:

> Gave healthful welcome to their shipwracked guests,
> And would have reft the fishers of their prey,
> Had not their bark been very slow of sail;   1.1.114

Separation seems final until, as years go by, one lost brother sets out to find the other.

Knowledge of the action of wind and tide, of buoyancy and methods of keeping afloat, together with the accurate use of sea terms, gives realism to this short sea narrative in verse.

Means of survival, following a wreck, are described in *Twelfth Night*:

> after our ship did *split*,
> When you, and those poor number saved with you
> Hung on our *driving boat*, I saw your brother,
> Most provident in peril, bind himself—
> Courage and hope both teaching him the practice—
> To a strong *mast* that *lived* upon the sea;

> Where, like Arion on a dolphin's back,
> I saw him hold acquaintance with the waves
> So long as I could see.   1.2.9 ff.

This, again, is realistic in fact and in wording. To "live" *upon*
or *in* the sea is, in seaphrase, to keep afloat, and a "driving boat"
is one that is being carried before the wind. The reference to
Arion on a dolphin's back, classical though it be, is neither out of
place nor out of character, for Antonio is not an unlettered sea
rover, but captain, formerly, of a ship of reprisal, with reading
and accomplishments in keeping with that.[1]

After the cry, "we split", goes up in *The Tempest*, all but the
mariners plunge "in the foaming brine", and the ways in which
they reach shore in safety are varied. Ferdinand, the prince, as
befits his character, strikes out and swims strongly. The King and
his party, "buoyed up by their sustaining garments", come
miraculously to land to make the best of life as castaways. The
drunken butler, by design it would seem rather than by accident,
escapes "upon a butt of sack which the sailors heaved overboard", and Trinculo declares that he has "swum ashore . . . like
a duck".[2]

Yet another survivor is Pericles. When his ship is "wrackt and
split", he is cast on the rocks, then, numbed and wet, makes his
way to some fishermen who aid him. His plight, and the cold and
exposure he has endured, make him a typical shipwrecked seafarer of the times:

> A man thronged up with cold, my veins are chill,
> And have no more of life than may suffice
> To give my tongue that heat to ask your help.   2.1.73

In *The Winter's Tale*, a wreck is described as it is taking place:

> I would you did but see how it chafes, how it rages, how it takes up the
> shore! But that's not to the point. O, the most piteous cry of the poor souls!
> sometimes to see 'em, and not to see 'em: now the ship boring the moon
> with her main-mast, and anon swallowed with yest and froth, as you'd
> thrust a cork into a hogs-head. . . . But to make an end of the ship, to see
> how the sea flap-dragoned it: but first, how the poor souls roared, and the
> sea mocked them: *W. Tale* 3.3.88

The might of the ocean leaves the onlooker astonished and
awestruck, but the cry of the distressed moves him most as his
direct, unforced words show. Pity overcomes every other feeling.
Humanitarianism is strong in the narratives of the Elizabethan
voyagers, and in Hakluyt himself as he reflects: "When I call to

---

[1] See p. 50.   [2] See Swimming, pp. 133-5.

minde, how many noble ships have bene lost, how many worthy
persons have bene drenched in the sea."[1] Official orders and
reports show it too, and it is noteworthy that nothing made the
Spaniards more abhorred than their callousness and their
cruelty.

The "direful spectacle" of what appears to be a wreck touches
"the very virtue of compassion" in Miranda also:

> O, I have suffered
> With those that I saw suffer! a brave vessel,
> Who had, no doubt, some noble creature in her,
> Dash'd all to pieces. O, the cry did knock
> Against my very heart! Poor souls, they perished!
> Had I been any god of power, I would
> Have sunk the sea within the earth, or ere
> It should the good ship so have swallowed, and
> The fraughting souls within her   1.2.5 ff.

But Prospero reassures her:

> Be collected:
> No more amazement: tell your piteous heart
> There's no harm done.   1.2.13

The cruel fate of being cast adrift is part of the story of the sea
and, near the end of Shakespeare's life, the most tragic tale of all
was that of the great explorer Henry Hudson. What it can mean
is finely imagined in a few lines that pass rapidly from conspiracy
and ruthless inhumanity to a forlorn scene of desolateness and
helplessness made more intense by a pathos that can trace
sympathy in the behaviour of the winds.

> they hurried us *aboard a bark*,
> Bore us some *leagues* to sea; where they prepared
> A rotten *carcass* of a butt, not *rigg'd*,
> Nor *tackle*, *sail* nor *mast*: the very rats
> Instinctively have quit it: there they *hoist* us,
> To cry to the sea that roar'd to us; to sigh
> To the winds, whose pity, sighing back again,
> Did us but loving wrong.   1.2.144

The sea terms and technical terms are realistic and accurate
and set off the sensibility and flight of fancy at the end, and
through them two contrasted worlds are made to face one
another.

Hakluyt, Vol. I (1903), XXXV.

PIRATES

The pirates that appear in Shakespeare are not like those found in sensational tales but are a reminder that piracy was one of the great evils of the age. Proclamations and edicts against them were frequent throughout the reigns of Elizabeth and James and these are echoed in the plays:

"Pitying therfore greatlie many of her owne subjects, who by theis spoiles have bene utterlie undone, and weighing besides howe dishonorable it is to her Majestie to suffer theis seas . . . to be by such leude persons haunted . . . (Her Majestie) thought it most necessarie for remedie therof to set out certaine of her shippes . . . for the cleereing of the seas and th' apprehension of the said Malefactors."[1]

A picture of what was happening is given in 2 *Henry VI* and, in its way, is almost like an appeal against it:[2]

> Pirates make cheap pennyworths of their pillage,
> And purchase friends, and give to courtezans,
> Still revelling like lords till all be gone;
> While as the silly owner of the goods
> Weeps over them, and wrings his hapless hands,
> And shakes his head, and trembling stands aloof,
> While all is shared and all is borne away,
> Ready to starve, and dare not touch his own: 1.1.222

Hamlet's encounter with pirates, far from being made up of wild and reckless daring in which chance plays the chief part, is a well-ordered incident which shows accurate knowledge of their tactics:

Ere we were two days old at sea, a pirate of very warlike appointment gave us chase. Finding ourselves too slow of sail, we put on a compelled valour: and in the grapple I boarded them: on the instant they got clear of our ship: so I alone became their prisoner. They have dealt with me like thieves of mercy: but they knew what they did: I am to do a good turn for them.
4.6.15

---

[1] *Documents Relating to Law and Custom of the Sea*, edited by R. G. Marsden, Navy Records Society, Vol. I, (1915), p. 210.
[2] See also 2 *Hen. VI* 4.9.33; *Rich. III* 1.3.158; *M. of V.* 1.3.22.

This is an exact report in strict nautical terms and official in style. It gives, in outline, a clear account of what took place and leaves out nothing that is essential for understanding every stage of the engagement. The pirates give chase. Hamlet's ship is slow of sail, but, rather than yield, he decides to "put on a compelled valour". This is a courageous and at the same time an astute move. It takes the pirates by surprise for "the roving pirate assaults not where he expects a firm resistance".[1] Grappling follows. Hamlet impetuously leads the assault and boards. To prevent others from following in his support, the pirates get clear "on the instant", with Hamlet as their prisoner. The tactics of both ships in grappling, boarding and falling off have been sound for, "It is a good stratagem to board a ship though she presently fall off again."[2] This way of getting clear is not invented by Shakespeare as a convenient way round an awkward point in the story. He uses a recognised stratagem to make it possible for Hamlet's ship to continue the voyage to England while Hamlet himself remains in the hands of the pirates who enable him to make a surprise return to Denmark.

The "good turn" that Hamlet is to do for them is connected with other measures of the time. Proclamations offering pardons were not infrequent in the Queen's reign and were issued regularly after 1603. Despite King James's "inward and essential detestation of that lawless and execrable course of life", it was his policy to encourage pirates to apply for a pardon, "considering . . . that a rigorous proceeding is not always the best means to reclaim men that are desperate, and that the hope of grace may make those become good subjects who are nothing moved with the terror of punishment".[3] In this way, the episode is kept realistic and up to date right to the end.[4]

Imprisonment was reserved for those not willing to amend, and in *Measure for Measure*, Ragozine is described as "a most notorious pirate" to explain his being in prison. His death from a "cruel fever" while there, "an accident that heaven provides", offers a way out of increasing difficulties (4.3.68 ff).

A brief snatch of pirate talk is heard in *Pericles*. Three rush in and, melodramatically, are only just in time to save Marina from death at the hands of a hired assassin:

[1] Boteler, p. 4.
[2] Monson, Vol. V, p. 148.
[3] Monson, Vol. III, pp. 376–78.
[4] *Hamlet*, S.R. 1602, Q1, 1603, Q2, 1605.

First. Hold villain!
Second. A prize! a prize!
Third. Half part, mates, half part. Come let's have her aboard suddenly.

4.1.97

"These roguing thieves serve the great pirate Valdes," they are not, like those in *Hamlet*, "thieves of mercy".

In *Antony and Cleopatra*, Shakespeare includes from Plutarch a picture of piracy in the ancient world which has a striking likeness to what was taking place in his own day, and that may in part be why he does so:

> Menecrates and Menas, famous pirates,
> Make the sea serve them, which they ear and wound
> With keels of every kind: many hot inroads
> They make in Italy: the borders maritime
> Lack blood to think on't, and flush youth revolt:
> No vessel can put forth, but 't is as soon
> Taken as seen; 1.4.48

There were unending complaints from English merchants about their losses in the Mediterranean and, from 1605, the danger from Mediterranean raiders who sometimes broke into the Narrow Seas, caused uneasiness in London. One corsair made his way as far up the Thames as Leigh in Essex before being taken.[1] Petitions which reached the King through Henry Wriothesley, Earl of Southampton, at last led him to consider sending out a fleet to suppress the pirate stronghold at Algiers. "The inhabitants consist principally of desperate rogues and renegadoes, that live by rapine, theft, and spoil, having renounced God and all virtue and become reprobates to all the Christian world."[2] Howard of Effingham, the hero of the Armada, by this time the aged Earl of Nottingham, was thought of at one stage for command of the expedition but it was delayed until 1620 and then ill-managed.

Another incident that caused much stir at the time may have suggested some burlesque at one point in *The Tempest*.

A notorious pirate, Thomas Salkeld, after plundering in the Bristol Channel, landed at Lundy with his crew of sixteen on 23 March 1609/10, and proclaimed himself king of the island. Monson, who as Admiral Commanding the Narrow Seas was sent out against him, declared, "I have never known villain so desperately bent against his countrymen, compelling them to

[1] *Letters of George*, Lord Carew, Camden Society, Vol. 76, p. 51.
[2] Monson, Vol. III, p. 86.

E

forswear their allegiance to his Majesty."[1] His tyrannous rule did
not last long for one of his prisoners, George Escott, an officer in
a Bridgewater coaster, showing great spirit, led a mutiny. Salkeld
fled and Escott was rewarded with a pension for recovering the
island.

Ludicrous parody of part of this seems to underlie the exchanges between Prospero and the drunken butler Stephano who,
with his loot and stolen goods, has attempted to set up as "King
of the island". Aching and bedraggled, he is whimsically asked:

> "You'ld be King o' the isle, sirrah?"

and he has humour and grace enough to reply:

> "I should have been a sore one, then."   5.1.288

Salkeld met his end at sea at the hands of a fellow pirate who
had him thrown overboard.

PIRATES AND PRIVATEERS

The Spaniards "have good cause to remember, how they were
baited in the Queenes time: there being never lesse then 200 sayle
of voluntaries and others, upon their coastes".[2]

Antonio in *Twelfth Night* has much in common with those
voluntaries who took part in irregular fighting at sea either at
their own expense or on a subsidy from merchant interests, and
he is also like those who, after the peace of 1603, continued a
war of their own against Spain maintaining that, as they spared
the ships of their fellow countrymen, they could not with justice
be charged with piracy.

Bold and venturesome, he follows the more daring tactics of
the time by grappling and boarding even when the odds happen
to be very unequal, and his enemies cannot but admit his valour

> such scathful grapple did he make
> With the most noble bottom of our fleet,
> That very envy and the tongue of loss
> Cried fame and honour on him.   5.1.55

The Spaniards, dismayed and discomfited though they might
be, are sometimes found speaking with much the same astonished
admiration of the feats of Drake and his men.

---

[1] Monson, Vol. III, p. 350.
[2] John Hagthorpe, *England's Exchequer* (1625), p. 25.

Nor is this Antonio's only exploit. He had seized a merchant-ship and its cargo and then engaged a man o' war, the *Tiger*:

> this is that Antonio
> That took the Phoenix and her fraught from Candy,
> And this is he that did the Tiger board,
> When your young nephew Titus lost his leg: 5.1.59

Finally, he is taken prisoner ashore as sometimes happened to English seamen in raids on Cadiz, Seville or Spanish settlements in the Indies:

> Here in the streets, desperate of shame and state,
> In private brabble did we apprehend him.

Orsino angrily addresses him as:

> "Notable pirate! thou salt water thief!"

Antonio, as captain of a ship of reprisal, is outraged:

> Be pleased that I shake off these names you give me;
> Antonio never yet was thief or pirate,
> Though, I confess, on base and ground enough,
> Orsino's enemy.

This is not a quibble, but a point that was much debated and stoutly contested by those who sailed without Letters of Marque from the Crown in Elizabeth's day, and even more so by those who defied the Proclamation of 1603 in which the King made plain:

"At our entering into these kingdomes of England and Ireland, we stood, as we still doe, in good amitie and friendship with all princes in Christendome.

Yet we are not ignorant that our late dear sister, the late Queene of England, had of long time warres with the King of Spaine, and during that time gave licences and commissions to divers of her and our now subjects, to set out and furnish to sea at their charges divers ships warlikely appointed, for the surprizing and taking of the said King's subjects and goods, and for the enjoying of the same, being taken and brought home, as lawful prize."

But the Proclamation went on to state that while "venturing their lives and goods for the weakening of the publicke enemie, and benefiting this their countrey" had been laudable and lawful in the past, it could be so no longer.[1]

[1] *Law and Custom of the Sea*, Vol. I, pp. 342–44. The lines would gain in force after 1603.

This did not please the privateers, and many of them continued their attacks at sea, holding like Antonio that, "on base and ground enough", they remained the enemies of Spain.

But though he "shakes off" the name of pirate, Antonio had been sailing in the kind of vessel that pirates were known to prefer: "roomy Ships, floaty, and of small charge",[1] or in other words, light, manoeuvrable and of shallow draught, and his accusers do not overlook this:

> A bawbling vessel was he captain of,
> For shallow draught and bulk unprizable; 5.1.52

After capturing ships, pirates would use "all art and industry to make [them] better sailers than all other ships. To this purpose they first cut down their half decks, and all other weighty things over head which make them wind-tight and burthensome; . . . they carry no weight over head, or in hold, but victuals, by means whereof and all these things considered no ship is able to equal them in going".[2]

A ship cut down in this way, though fast sailing, would no longer have good sea keeping qualities and could thus be said to be "bawbling". It met the need of the moment and was not meant to last. "They never regard the strength of their ships more than for one voyage, for they want not continual prizes which they take of Christians and thus use."[2]

Much is therefore implied in "bawbling" and also in the description "for . . . bulk unprizable". Bulk is the sea term for cargo. To "break bulk" is to break into the cargo. This vessel would carry little or none—"they carry no weight . . . in hold but victuals"—and so for its bulk or cargo would not be worth taking as a prize. The same holds good if "bulk" is used in the sense of frame, body or hull, for a ship so much reduced would be of little further value.

If, on the other hand, speed and shallow draught are to be stressed, then a vessel that was fast-sailing and able to work in shallow water could easily elude capture as a prize and would be unprizable in this very different sense. But this would give the word an unusual and rather strained meaning.

[1] Mainwaring, Vol. II, p. 25.   [2] Monson, Vol. III, p. 267.

OFFICERS BELONGING TO
A ROYAL SHIP

"We will propound all the distinct officers belonging to a royal ship of war; and consider of all their particular charges and duties." Boteler, 11.

ADMIRAL

The Admiral is of first rank and command in a fleet. In Elizabethan days, soldiers of high rank might be given charge of expeditions by sea, and the titles admiral and general were interchangeable. Monson gives his views on this: "There have been often disputes, whether the title of Admiral or General were more proper to a sea commander; and though I dare not presume to conclude of either, yet I think it is as improper to call an Admiral a General by sea, as to call a General an Admiral by land."[1]

It does not affect Shakespeare who mentions only three admirals. One is English: "Richmond is their admiral", and two are French, the Admiral of France slain at Agincourt (*Hen. V* 4.8.95), and the "high admiral" in 3 *Henry VI* (3.3.252). The Elizabethan practice was to call the flagship "the admiral", and Shakespeare follows this, referring to the Egyptian flagship, the *Antoniad*, as "the Egyptian admiral" (3.10.2). Falstaff also uses admiral in the sense of the admiral's ship.[2] In Drake's *Voyage*, his ship is referred to as the admiral and he himself as the general: "the admirall (wherein our generall himself went)."[3]

CAPTAIN

"A captain is chosen for his warlike part, as the master is for the conduction of his ship."[4]

In other words, the captain was an officer put on board to be

[1] Monson, Vol. III, p. 438.
[2] See p. 68.
[3] *The World Encompassed*, Hakluyt Society (1854), p. 8.
[4] Monson, Vol. IV, p. 152.

in command and to direct all sea fights, and the master was in charge of the sailing of the ship.

There were two main types of captain. One chosen by an admiral or general for command of a warship, another of less standing in charge of a ship of reprisal and authorised "to arrest by all means . . . the vessels of his enemy".[1] Antonio in *Twelfth Night* is a captain of this latter sort. Pericles is in full command of a royal ship which has a master and a boatswain, but he gives the orders for shaping course and, in an emergency, helps with the working of the ship.

Alonso in *The Tempest* is also a king but, unlike Pericles, never takes charge though he does come on deck to find out what is happening: "Where's the master?", and to exhort the mariners, "Play the men". This phrase, though now found only in the form "play the man", is a usual Elizabethan one for "be men", "act like men".

> "And the Portugals, peradventure encouraged by our slack working, played the men; and had Barricadoes made where they might stand without any danger of our shot."[2]

LIEUTENANT

Originally, the title of lieutenant was given to one officer only, the captain's understudy, or second in command in a fighting ship. "The Lieutenant is to associate the Captaine."[3] Shakespeare gives some prominence to the rank at a time when it was much discussed and when there was strong support for establishing it and making it permanent. Howard considered that lieutenants could not be done without. "There is here in our fleet many lieutenants and corporals, which of necessity we were and are driven to have," and he was ready to meet part of the cost himself. "The matter, it is not great in respect of the service. I think 500 l., with the help of my own purse, will do it; but howsoever it fall out I must see them paid, and will." Howard felt that this should not be an arrangement for emergencies only. "I do not look to end with this service, and therefore I must be followed hereafter. My good Lord, look but what the

---

[1] Monson, Vol. IV, p. 17.
[2] *Voyages and Travels* (An English Garner), Vol. II (1903), p. 147.
[3] *A Sea Grammar*, by John Smith (1627), p. 36.

officers had with Sir Francis Drake, having but 4 of her Majesty's ships. I do not desire half so much for all this great fleet."[1] This was written from the *Ark Royal* in Dover Road, on 26 August 1588. The decisive battle against the Armada had already been fought off Gravelines on 29 July, but there was still need for vigilance.

Shakespeare, as has been seen, shows what a lieutenant's duties include, and how responsible they can be, in a notable scene in 2 *Henry VI*, on which he may have been at work only a year after the defeat of the Armada.[2]

"A Captain is to make choice of his lieutenant."[3] Appointment to the rank depended so much on a captain's preference and sometimes on his willingness to make good the sum for a lieutenant's pay that many had their hopes dashed, and the feelings of chagrin that could arise are voiced in Iago's bitter words. Iago serves by sea and land and, "a Lieutenant's place at sea in respect of hope and command, is as the Lieutenant's place at land".[4] Canvassing by friends comes first:

> Three great ones of the city,
> In personal suit to make me his lieutenant,
> Off-capped to him: and, by the faith of man,
> I know my price, I am worth no worse a place:　1.1.8 ff.

Then, as often happened:

> But he, as loving his own pride and purposes,
> Evades them, with a bombast circumstance
> Horribly stuffed with epithets of war:
> And, in conclusion,
> Nonsuits my mediators; for, "Certes", says he,
> "I have already chose my officer".

A smarting sense of injured merit follows:

> And what was he?
> Forsooth a great mathematician,
> One Michael Cassio,

In Iago's view an "arithmetician" is a "bookish theoric", one given to "mere prattle without practice". But the great advances in navigation in Shakespeare's day were made possible by the mathematicians, and for Othello to prefer one would seem very reasonable then. Cassio later sails in his squadron against the Turks.

These are discontents of the time, and Shakespeare makes use

---

[1] *Defeat of the Spanish Armada*, Vol. II, pp. 165–66. (Howard: postscript to a letter of John Hawkyns to Burghley.)
[2] See pp. 4–5.　　[3] Monson, Vol. IV, p. 15.　　[4] Boteler, p. 32.

of them in this original[1] way as one of the mainsprings of the drama.

There is a burlesque of the rank, and also of the method of appointment to it, in *The Tempest* where Stephano promises Caliban:

> "thou shalt be my Lieutenant Monster, or
> my standard."   3.2.14

THE CORPORAL

The corporal "is to see the soldiers and sailors keep their arms neat, clean, and yare, and to teach and exercise them every calm day, sometimes with shot, and sometimes with false fires".[2]

Boteler, who speaks of the rank as "late introduced" when he ought to say re-introduced (for Howard had appointed corporals in 1588) sees it as a very necessary rank "especially to the perfecting of the practice of fiery weapons. And withal it may lead, in a fit way, towards the making of a Lieutenant; and therefore I shall advise at sea, that these Corporals might be gentlemen; nor is there any cause why a gentleman should scorn the place."[3]

Unlike the lieutenant, no corporal in the plays does the rank any credit. In the *Merry Wives of Windsor* and *Henry V*, there is Corporal Nym who serves at sea as well as by land. Elsewhere,[4] corporals have only passing mention in connection with land service.

THE GUNNER

> The master, the swabber, the boatswain, and I,
> The gunner, and his mate. *Temp.* 2.2.47

Except in this sea catch sung by Stephano, the gunner at sea is not heard of. Much was required of him, "for the strength of the ship is put into his hands".[5]

Nor were his duties confined to gunnery. "A principal thing in a gunner at sea is to be a good helmsman and to call to him at helm to loof, or bear up, to have his better level, and to observe the heaving and setting of the sea to take his aim at the enemy."[5]

Stephano repeats the helmsman's call "bear up" when ashore.[6]

---

[1] There is nothing of this in his source.   [2] Monson, Vol. IV, p. 58.   [3] Boteler, p. 32.
[4] 1 *Hen. IV* 4.2.26; 2 *Hen. IV* 2.4.166, 3.2.288. *L.L.L.* 3.1.189.
[5] Monson, Vol. IV, p. 33.   [6] See Helm, p. 107.

THE MASTER

"The office of a master is to guide a ship into what coast, height, or harbour the captain shall direct him, who is commander of all; and in a fight is to con the ship, and to see the handling of the sails, by appointment of the captain.

"A master must be obedient to his captain, and so carry himself, that he be obeyed by his company."[1]

It was very important that captain and master should work together in harmony though this did not always happen. Boteler speaks of masters "who undergo the command of a Captain over them with a great deal of grudging and sullenness".[2] But tributes to their skill, worth and high sense of duty are frequent.

"I should do the master of my ship wrong if I should not further his careful service, being a man of substance, most valiant, and most sufficient besides concerning his charge. I would desire you to prefer him to her Majesty coat of ordinary, for I know ne'er a man in England that I would wish sooner to have care of the prince's person, if they were driven to the seas, than him."[3]

The Master in Othello's ship is commended much in this way at the end of the perilous voyage.

> Bring thou the master to the citadel;
> He is a good one, and his worthiness
> Does challenge much respect.   2.1.210

In *The Tempest*, the Master has a double responsibility, the safety of the King and Prince, and the safety of the ship. He is seen running the ship according to the chain of command laid down for royal ships and vessels of war.

"The whole ship's company is divided, both in respect of the labour and command, into two parts; the boatswain and all the common sailors under his command, to be before the mainmast; the Captain, master, master's mate, gunners, quartermasters, trumpeters, etc., to be abaft the mainmast."[4]

This being so, the Master in *The Tempest* first sees that all is well "up for'ard" where the boatswain is in charge.[5] He then goes aft

[1] Monson, Vol. IV, p. 24.   [2] Boteler, p. 31.
[3] *Defeat of the Spanish Armada*, Vol. II, p. 127. (Seymour to Walsyngham, 18 August 1588.)
[4] Mainwaring, Vol. II, pp. 86–87.   [5] See Boatswain, pp. 58–60.

to direct the overall working of the ship, giving orders on his silver whistle which the Boatswain interprets: "Tend to the master's whistle." When the King comes on deck and asks where the Master is, the answer, "do you not hear him?" from the Boatswain, indicates that all is under control.

This division of command "into two parts" is adhered to in Prospero's later order to Ariel:

> the master and the boatswain
> Being awake, enforce them to this place;   5.1.99

He does not send for the Master alone.

At the end, when all is well, the Master is heard of once more, surveying his ship with pride, and "capering to eye her" (5.1.238).

The office of master kept its importance in warships until the end of the days of sail, and on board the *Victory* at Trafalgar, the structure of command had links with the old tradition.

COMMANDER IN CHIEF: Vice Admiral Lord Nelson.
CAPTAIN: Thomas Masterman Hardy.
MASTER: Thomas Atkinson.

In merchant ships, the Master was in full charge. He was often owner as well as navigator.

> Her husband's to Aleppo gone, master o' the Tiger:
> Though his bark cannot be lost,
> Yet it shall be tempest-tost.   *Macbeth* 1.3.7 ff.

THE BOATSWAIN

"This officer must needs be of much use and necessity for the due disciplining, and ordering of the whole company belonging to the ship; and it behoves him to be stirring, stout and faithful."[1]

The qualities and skill required in a good boatswain and the nature of his duties are very well understood by Shakespeare, and his study of a character many-sided but consistent is lifelike. "His and his mate's work is never at an end, for it is impossible to repeat all the offices that are put upon them."[2] He is "to call up every man to his labour and office",[2] and this he is set to do by the Master in the opening scene of *The Tempest*. He shows himself a correct subordinate officer:

[1] Boteler, p. 16.   [2] Monson, Vol. IV, p. 33.

Master.   Boatswain!
Boatswain. Here, master: what cheer?
Master.   Good:[1] speak to th' mariners: fall to 't, yarely, or we run
               ourselves aground: bestir, bestir.

He takes charge straight away:

"Heigh, my hearts! cheerly, cheerly my hearts!"

Then "upon the winding of the master's whistle, the boatswain takes it with his, and sets the sailors with courage to do their work, every one of them knowing by their whistle what they are to do".[2] This, once more, is what happens:

"Yare, yare! Take in the topsail. Tend to th' master's whistle."

He has excellent power of command, putting heart into his men as he gives orders. All do their utmost for all are working as one.

With Alonso's panic-stricken and troublesome courtiers who are getting in the way, the Boatswain is firm and is no respecter of persons:

"You mar our labour: keep your cabins: you do assist the storm."

With Gonzalo, the King's counsellor, he is aware of his own authority and his downrightness and common sense add to it:

"You are a counsellor; if you can command these elements to silence ... we will not hand a rope more; use your authority: if you cannot, give thanks you have lived so long, and make yourself ready in your cabin for the mischance of the hour, if it so hap."

From this and his remark, "What cares these roarers for the name of King? To cabin: silence! trouble us not", he has been thought a leveller at heart. But he is neither a revolutionary nor one who prides himself on taking liberties or on being unceremonious. He is doing no more than his duty and is carrying out strictly what belongs to his office. For the duties of a boatswain included those of a Master at Arms, who is charged with supervising the ship's discipline and has power "to commit all offenders". With the courtiers, who are offensive as well as interfering, he is the ship's police:

"Yet again! what do you here? Shall we give o'er, and drown? Have you a mind to sink?"

Nor is there any question of his loyalty. His words to the King, spoken under stress, are respectful:

"I pray now, keep below."

[1] A superior acknowledged a report or an answer in this way. Today "very good" is used.

He reserves, "Out of our way, I say", for the others. Moreover, his loyalty breaks out spontaneously near the end of the play:

> The best news is, that we have safely found
> Our King, and company;[1] the next, our ship —— 5.1.222

The King comes first.

His efforts for the safety of the ship and its company are tireless.

Accounts of the traditional duties of a boatswain were not published till after Shakespeare's time, but they confirm what he portrays.

THE TRUMPETER

"For the more reputation of this man's service in a ship of the King's, and under an Admiral, it is fit he should have a silver trumpet, and himself and his noise to have banners of silk of the Admiral's colours. His place is to keep the poop, to attend the General's going ashore and coming aboard, and all other strangers or boats, and to sound as an entertainment to them; as also when they hail a ship, or when they charge, board, or enter her."[2]

Ceremony of this kind is carried out in Pompey's galley when Augustus Caesar and his company are banqueting aboard, and as they go ashore.

Trumpeters serving with land forces appear in 1 *Henry VI*:

> Go to the gates of Bordeaux, trumpeter;
> Summon their general unto the wall 4.2.1

and again in *Antony and Cleopatra*,

> Trumpeters,
> With brazen din blast you the city's ear; 4.8.35

THE SWABBER

The Swabber's "office and charge is, to make and keep the ship clean, and that as well in the great cabin as everywhere betwixt the decks; to which (end) he hath also a mate or two allowed him, according to the burthen and bigness of the ship".[3]

It was not a coveted office and could be a form of punishment.

---

[1] Ship's company is the royal naval term for the whole company, officers, men and boys, in H.M. ships.
[2] Monson, Vol. IV, p. 57.   [3] Boteler, p. 11.

'No man shall play at cards or dice either for his apparel or arms upon pain of being disarmed and made a swabber of the ship."[1]

When Viola in *Twelfth Night* addresses Maria as "good swabber",[2] the affront is not lost on Olivia who remarks with some reproach, "Sure you have some hideous matter to deliver, when the courtesy of it is so fearful," and Maria's resentment continues for some time.

THE SURGEON

Royal ships carried surgeons "exempted from all duty but to attend the sick and cure the wounded".[3]

Though a ship's surgeon does not appear in any of the plays, a physician stands by to help those who have suffered shipwreck in *Pericles*, and it is by his skill that the Queen is revived when the caulked and bitumed chest, in which she lies apparently lifeless, has been washed ashore. Here, as the physician of noble birth is shown at his tasks, Shakespeare pays his great tribute to the selflessness, the compassion, the patience through long vigils, of those who are dedicated to the art of healing:

> But I much marvel that your lordship, having
> Rich tire about you, should at these early hours
> Shake off the golden slumber of repose.
> 'Tis most strange,
> Nature should be so conversant with pain,
> Being thereto not compelled.   3.2.21 ff.

From the physician who sets his calling and skill above rank and wealth comes the answer:

> I hold it ever,
> Virtue and cunning* were endowments greater   *skill
> Than nobleness* and riches: careless heirs   *rank
> May the two latter darken and expend,
> But immortality attends the former,
> Making a man a god.

The shipwrecked have attention first:

> Get fire and meat for these poor men.   3.2.3

In his dispensary are those who have come for relief for themselves:

> Give this to the 'pothecary,
> And tell me how it works,   3.2.9

---

[1] *Fighting Instructions 1530–1816*, pp. 43–44.   [2] See Hull, pp. 106–7.
[3] Monson, Vol. IV, p. 57.

or who seek help for others:

> Your master will be dead ere you return;
> There's nothing can be ministered to nature
> That can recover him.   3.2.7

He knows from what he has been told of the state of the sufferer
that there is no longer any hope.

    The reviving of the Queen "by good appliance" follows, and it
lends itself to drama:

> For look how fresh she looks! They were too rough
> That threw her in the sea. Make a fire within;
> Fetch hither all my boxes in my closet.
> Death may usurp on nature many hours,
> And yet the fire of life kindle again
> The o'erpress'd spirits.   3.2.81

Music, because of its restorative effect, is called for:

> The rough and woeful music that we have,
> Cause it to sound, beseech you.
> The viol once more:— how thou stirr'st, thou block!
> The music there! I pray you, give her air.   3.2.90

Gradually the Queen begins to "blow into life's flower again", to
the astonishment and admiration of the attendants:

> The heavens through you, increase our wonder,
> And set up your fame forever.   3.2.97

But all is not yet well, and great care must be taken still:

>   Hush, my gentle neighbours!
> Lend me your hands; to the next chamber bear her.
> Get linen: now this matter must be looked to,
> For her relapse is mortal. Come, come;
> And Aesculapius guide us!   3.2.110

These last words addressed to divine powers that preside over
healing, "Aesculapius guide us," show the humility of one who
looks on skill as a trust.

SEAMEN AND BOYS

SEAMEN

"The bred seaman is for the most part hardy and undaunted, ready to adventure any desperate action, be it good or bad ... The seamen's desire is to be commanded by those that understand their labour laws and customs ... The seamen are stubborn or perverse when they perceive their commander is ignorant of the discipline of the sea, and cannot speak to them in their own language."[1]

Shakespeare sees them in this way and shows their hardihood, courage and skill, their cheerfulness, goodfellowship and civility: their discipline and deep attachment to the ways of the sea.

In *The Tempest*, they carry out their hard tasks in silence with a control that is impressive amid the fury of the storm. In *Hamlet*, they make a brief appearance and bring with them a healthy and welcome world. "Seafaring men, sir, they say they have letters for you." Their greeting is traditional: "God bless you, sir."[2] It is returned with "Let Him bless thee too," which prompts a further, "He shall, sir, an't please Him." This is not an exaggeration of their style for, in eyewitness reports by voyagers, "it pleased God" is often repeated at every fresh happening no matter how rapidly one may follow another.[3] Their message is delivered in a forthright manner and with an exactness that shows training: "There's a letter for you, sir, it comes from th' ambassador that was bound for England, if your name be Horatio, as I am let to know it is."[4] The same precise way of answering questions or acknowledging orders is seen in *Pericles*.

Pericles.	Mariner, say what coast is this?
Sailor.	We are near Tharsus.
Pericles.	Thither, gentle mariner,
	Alter thy course for Tyre. When canst thou reach it?
Sailor.	By break of day, if the wind cease. 3.1.72

[1] Monson, Vol. III, p. 434.
[2] Also in *Pericles*, "What courage, sir? God save you!" 3.1.38.
[3] *Three Voyages of Martin Frobisher*, Hakluyt Society (1867), pp. 296–300.
[4] *Hamlet* 4.6.1 ff.

"Alter" is the correct naval term; "change" is never used for alterations of course.

This characteristic style is continued in the later harbour scene when messages are being taken or passed on.[1]

Their skill and endurance are best seen in the storm scenes in *The Tempest* and *Pericles* where lesser instances also occur of their practical efficiency: "Sir, we have a chest beneath the hatches, caulked and bitumed ready" *Per.* (3.1.70). Unexpected reminders of their ways and day to day life lend colour or force to retorts and arguments:

> "He would pun thee into shivers with his fist, as
> a sailor breaks a biscuit"

is Thersites's heartening assurance to Ajax in *Troilus and Cressida* (2.1.43). Their bread, called biscuit, was specially made and dried to an unusual hardness to ensure that it would keep. Jaques finds the wit of Touchstone "as dry as the remainder biscuit After a voyage" (*A.Y.L.* 2.7.39).

Arviragus in *Cymbeline* speaks of "winds that sailors rail at" (4.2.57), and this they are heard doing: "Blow till thou burst thy wind"; "blow and split thyself".[2] Their daily speech is brought in, sometimes where it is not looked for:

Polonius. My lord, I have news to tell you.
Hamlet.   Buz, buz! 2.2.398

Among seamen in the Royal Navy it is still an everyday practice when passing on a rumour or whispered news, to begin with the words "Buzz, buzz!", which invite attention to what is about to be said. A way of asking for news is to say: "What's the latest buzz?"

The traditions of the sea rule their lives and, if need be, are proudly asserted:

> "Pardon us, sir; with us at sea it hath been still observed: and we
> are strong in custom." *Per.* 3.1.51

In mishap and disaster, they can jest at a doom that may be theirs any moment. A huge wave

> from the ladder-tackle washes off
> A canvas-climber, "Ha!" says one, "wilt out?" 4.1.60

From a fellow seaman who may share the same fate even while he speaks, it shows fatalism that is not unheroic, but it would not come well from anyone else.

---

[1] See p. 21.   [2] See pp. 38, 41.

In the naval regulations, times were appointed for worship:

"Because no action nor enterprise can prosper, be it by sea or by land, without the favour and assistance of Almighty God . . . , you shall not fail to cause divine service to be read in your ship morning and evening, in the morning before dinner and in the evening before supper, or at least (if there be interruption by foul weather) once in the day praising God every night with the singing of a psalm at the setting of the watch."[1]

The influence of this is seen in their greetings and in what they do in moments of danger. The Boatswain tells Gonzalo "give thanks you have lived so long, and make yourself ready in your cabin for the mischance of the hour, if it so hap", and the mariners in distress cry, "All lost! to prayers, to prayers."

Their less orderly ways are not forgotten. Hastings, who has put his faith in Richard III, has to confess to himself:

> Who builds his hope in air of your fair looks
> Lives like a drunken sailor on a mast,
> Ready with every nod to tumble down
> Into the fatal bowels of the deep. *R. III* 3.4.101

If things went wrong on board, soldiers and others taking passage would vent their feelings by charging the sailors, quite indiscriminately, with drunkenness. This standing taunt is freely hurled by the thwarted and impious Antonio in *The Tempest*: "We are merely cheated of our lives by drunkards." Trinculo, Stephano and their new acquaintance Caliban are later found ashore in a state that makes the charge unanswerable:

> where should they
> Find this grand liquor that hath gilded them?
> How cam'st thou in this pickle? 5.1.279

But, though in this and in their pillaging, they have taken to some of the discreditable ways of seamen, Stephano redeems himself by showing a true sense of the brotherhood of the sea as their bewilderment and recklessness increase:

> "Every man shift for all the rest, and let no man take care for himself; for all is but fortune." 5.1.256

"Last scene of all" is repose:

> The mariners all under hatches stow'd;
> ASLEEP *Temp.* 1.2.230

---

[1] *Fighting Instructions, 1530–1816*, edited by Julian S. Corbett, Navy Records Society (1905), p. 36.

F

The readiness of officers and men to acknowledge one another's good qualities, and to recognise that they could not do without one another, led to a sense of obligation on both sides and was a strong bond. It is seen in Lord Howard of Effingham:

> "as yet we are not troubled with any mutinies, nor I hope shall not; for I see men kindly handled will bear want and run through the fire and water."[1]

Roger Marbeck, at one time provost of Oriel College, Oxford, and later physician to the Lord Admiral during the Cadiz voyage of 1596, gives a picture of Howard's "honourable care no less for the good usage of all his followers of all sorts and degrees but especially for the poor toiling and continual labouring mariner, himself daily making inquiry how they did, and calling to them by name to know in what case they stood, and what they did lack, bidding them boldly to utter their wants and they should have present relief, so familiar in his honourable speeches, so affable, and well pleasing in his heroical countenance, so open handed in rewarding such as he saw diligent and painful in their labours, so bountiful in bestowing of gifts, where either any need or good desert was, so pleasant and courteous in provoking of them to some one kind of exercise or other at convenient times to keep them from idleness and sea distastes, a thing most necessary and of great moment in these kind of regiments, as I dare protest there was not one man there but would be as willing to venture his life at the command of so honourable a leader, as he would be to fall to his meat in the greatest time of his hunger".[2] The tradition remained unbroken. Shakespeare knew it well. It was Nelson's way. Pericles is shown as a commander who "understands their labour" and speaks "to them in their own language". And with the Boatswain, an officer of lower rank, it is the same.

BOYS

Boys were borne in royal ships, in privateers and merchantmen:

> Some to the wars, to try their fortune there;
> Some, to discover islands far away.   *T.G. of V.* 1.3.8

[1] *Defeat of the Spanish Armada*, Vol. I, p. 198.
[2] "A Breefe and a true Discourse of the late honorable voyage unto Spaine ..." by Roger Marbeck, British Museum, Sloane MS. 226, f. 11. (Spelling modernised.)

Spirited and mettlesome, dutiful and wayward by turns, they are seen at their tasks as the fleet puts to sea:

> Upon the hempen tackle ship-boys[1] climbing;
> Hear the shrill whistle which doth order give
> To sounds confused; *Hen. V* 3, Chor. 8

The call of the sea and eagerness "to see the wonders of the world abroad"[2] took them forth, and enabled them to make light of hardships.

Alone of its kind in all literature, and beyond the range of painter or any but the supreme artist in words, is the picture of the boy sailor "on the high and giddy mast", wet, overwatched and overcome by slumber, the envy of the careworn, wearied monarch whose eyelids sleep no more weighs down.

> Wilt thou upon the high and giddy mast
> Seal up the ship-boy's eyes and rock his brains
> In cradle of the rude imperious surge,
> And in the visitation of the winds,
> Who take the ruffian billows by the top,
> Curling their monstrous heads, and hanging them
> With deaf'ning clamour in the slippery clouds,
> That, with the hurly, death itself awakes?
> Canst thou, O partial sleep! give thy repose
> To the wet sea-boy in an hour so rude,
> And in the calmest and most stillest night,
> With all appliances and means to boot,
> Deny it to a king? 2 *Hen. IV* 3.1.18 ff.

Prince Arthur makes his fatal attempt to escape to freedom dressed like a sailor boy, a disguise that adds to his gallantness and that would endear him to an Elizabethan audience.

> The wall is high, and yet I will leap down.
> There's few or none do know me: if they did,
> This ship-boy's semblance hath disguised me quite. *K. John* 4.3.1

[1] This usage is correct: "the waggery and idleness of the ship boys paid by the Boatswain with the rod." Boteler, p.19.
[2] *T.G. of V.* 1.1.6.

SAILORS AND SEA-SOLDIERS

Before the Royal Marines were instituted by King Charles II, soldiers were carried aboard ships in all warlike expeditions. This had to be done even though it could give rise to difficulties; "it being generally known that land soldiers are not only impatient of sea sufferings, but withal very much given to mutinies, and violent distempers against seamen upon the least sense of hardship."[1] But they were under orders to work together as Raleigh's *Instructions*, based on precedent, make plain:

> "You shall cause all your landsmen to learn the names and places of the ropes, that they may assist the sailors in their labour upon the decks, though they cannot go up to the tops and yards."[2]

This is of great interest because it explains why professional soldiers like Enobarbus, Othello, Iago, Falstaff, Pistol are at times found talking like sailors and showing a readiness and exactness in the use of sea terms which is very different from any mere colouring of their talk with them. It may seem strange now, and the likeliness of it has been questioned, but there was nothing unusual in it in Shakespeare's day. In the same way, sailors could be used in operations ashore:

> "You shall train and instruct your sailors, so many as shall be found fit, as you do your landsmen, and register their names in the list of your companies, making no difference of professions, but that all be esteemed sailors and all soldiers, for your troops will be very weak when you come to land without the assistance of your seafaring men."

When Falstaff makes merry at the expense of Bardolph, whose face is like a ball of wildfire in the night, and says "thou art our admiral, thou bearest the lantern in the poop, but 'tis in

---

[1] Boteler, p. 63.   [2] *Fighting Instructions 1530–1816*, edited by Julian S. Corbett, Navy Records Society (1905), p. 37.

the nose of thee" (1 *Hen. IV*, 3.3.24), he is recalling the Fleet
order:

> The Admiral with his squadron are to sail in the front or van; that
> so he may lead the way to all the fleet in general, by the view of his flag
> in his main top, by day, and by his light or lanthorn in his poop in the
> night.[1]

The likeness breaks down because the poop is the aftermost part
of the upper deck and Bardolph's nose is not at the back of his
head, but Falstaff is quick to forestall being corrected.

In the *Merry Wives of Windsor*, Falstaff talks of his escapades as
sea adventures:

> they shall be my East and West Indies, and I will trade to them
> both. 1.3.72

He likens himself to a privateer in lawful command of a pinnace,
"with commission to take" as distinct from a pirate who "takes
without commission and makes all the world his enemies".[2]

> bear you these letters tightly:
> Sail like my pinnace to these golden shores. 1.3.78

This is a very artful way of trying to keep his standing and of
suggesting that there is nothing irregular in his actions. Falstaff's
use of these nautical parallels is not random, they are cleverly
worked out.

The lesser characters, who have been outwitting him, fall in
with his sea-talk and keep it running as far as intelligent novices
can be expected to do. They have only a few terms which many
landsmen would know, but they make the most of them and use
them aptly:

M. Page.   ... he would never have boarded me in this fury.
M. Ford.   Boarding, call you it? I'll be sure to keep him above deck.
M. Page.   So will I, if he come under my hatches, I'll never to sea again.
                                                          2.1.80–84

But, of particular interest is the way in which Pistol, another
of these sea-soldiers, chooses to announce that he means to win
the hostess, Mrs. Quickly, as his wife:

> This pink is one of Cupid's carriers.
> Clap on more sails; pursue; up with your fights;[3]
> Give fire! she is my prize, or ocean whelm them all! 2.2.134

Here, he gives the order for setting more sail and the words of
command for chase, opening fire, boarding and capture, with

---

[1] Boteler, p. 279.   See Admiral, p. 53, and Poop, p. 108.   [2] Monson, Vol. IV, p. 17.
[3] *Fights* were canvas screens to conceal men or to protect them from gunfire.   *Clap on*, see
p. 115; *give fire*, p. 118.

the accuracy of one who has served aboard an armed vessel. That he should refer to his future wife as a "Pink" is appropriate for several reasons. As lawful spoils of war these vessels were highly valued. "These commonly go well, and are of good burthen." Pirates were always on the watch for them, for, "being slightly manned", they were easily surprised.[1] Pistol, though he foresees some resistance, means this pursuit and capture to be conducted on honourable lines. The rules of an open and stout sea fight are to be kept in contrast to other methods of the day:

> "When small Pinks and little vessels do stop below Graves-end, in Tilbury Hope, or against Queenborough, the wind being westerly, they [the Pirates] may, with one or two wherries in the night, go aboard and enter them, and put to sea before a wind, so that they cannot be stayed or prevented.'[1]

[1] Mainwaring, Vol. II, pp. 14–15.

PILLAGE

Prospero's means of foiling the plot against his life, led by Caliban, has been thought a somewhat unreal device, either hastily contrived or borrowed perhaps from Italian Comedy. But the incident is not farfetched, nor does it owe anything to a foreign source. It is a lively, amusing, realistic account of what seamen of the day were known to be prone to, and it is very appropriate that it should be brought into this sea drama.

"As for the business of pillage, there is nothing that more bewitcheth them, nor anything wherein they promise to themselves so loudly nor delight in more mainly. Insomuch that I have known some of them . . . to rove into an enemy's quarter, three or four miles, in hope only to pillage some rotten household stuff. And I did see one of these make his brave retreat with a feather bed on his back, all that long way in an extremity of hot weather; although it was not worth ten shillings, when he had it home.

"Such is the extreme irregularity and bold madness of the common mariner and common officer too."[1]

Prospero makes good use of this known weakness to trap Trinculo and Stephano who are members of a royal ship's company and have come to share the seaman's mania for pillage:

Prospero.   The trumpery in my house, go bring it hither,
        For stale to catch these thieves. 4.1.186

It works at once as he had foreseen. Trinculo is unable to resist: "O worthy Stephano! look what a wardrobe here is for thee!" Their confederate Caliban is left astonished and dismayed, for he sees that all his plans will be upset. In vain he protests:

"Let it alone, thou fool; it is but trash."

As was usual, they begin to quarrel about what each is to have:

Stephano.   Put off that gown, Trinculo; by this hand, I'll have that gown.

---

[1] Boteler, pp. 37–41.

Caliban becomes desperate:

> The dropsy drown this fool! What do you mean
> To dote thus on such luggage? Let't alone,
> And do the murther first:

But they pay no heed, and go on to make a pack horse of him:

Stephano.   Monster, lay to your fingers: help to bear this away where my hogs-
head of wine is, or I'll turn you out of my kingdom: go to, carry this.
Trinculo.   And this.
Stephano.   Aye, and this.

In the end, these "straggling thieves for pillage fighting"[1] are suddenly set upon and hunted about by dogs and hounds as happened to shore raiders, returning laden to their ships, when the Spaniards let dogs loose on them.

Near the close, the King takes charge and commands them:

> "Hence, and bestow your luggage where you found it."   5.1.298

Boteler, with a view to recruitment, was prepared to make quite serious use of "the extravagancy of their hopes, in point of pillage", holding that it could be a strong inducement to "a willing employment of themselves" and that "the very noise and hearsay of such a grant shall not only entice them into these services, but make them adventurous and stout in fights, when they come to them".[2]

Shakespeare, before him, had turned it to very good account dramatically.

[1] *Lucrece*, 428.   [2] Boteler, p. 38.

TIDES

"Indeed it is one of the principal parts requirable in a good mariner, and especially frequenting our English coasts where the tides are both great and various, to know his tides and thoroughly to understand how they set from point to point; and withal to distinguish the difference of those in the open seas, and the largest channels, from those near the shores, and in creeks and rivers."[1]

The influence of the moon on the tides:

"The moist star,
Upon whose influence Neptune's empire stands," *Ham.* 1.1.118

was accepted in Shakespeare's day, though not properly understood until explained and defined mathematically by Sir Isaac Newton. "The fortune of us that are moon's men doth ebb and flow like the sea, being governed as the sea is by the moon," jests Prince Hal (1 *Hen. IV* 1.2.31), and Camillo's way of expressing the impossible is to say "you may as well Forbid the sea for to obey the moon" (*W.T.* 1.2.427). Sycorax could control the moon and so "make flows and ebbs" (*Temp.* 5.1.270).

But more important is the knowledge that Shakespeare shows of how the tides behave.

The term "tide" applies to the periodic rise and fall of the level of the sea, the heaping up and subsiding of the water. It is a vertical, up and down movement and is not to be confused with the "stream" which is a horizontal movement, the inflow and outflow caused by the rise and fall. The rising tide is called the flood tide, and it is accompanied by the flood stream. The falling tide is called the ebb tide and with it goes the ebb stream. Shakespeare is aware of what is at work.

This common body,
Like to a vagabond flag upon the stream,
Goes to and back, lackeying the varying tide,
To rot itself with motion. *Ant. and Cleo.* 1.4.47

Here, the stream is the alternating flood stream and ebb stream caused by the rise and fall of the tide, "lackeying the varying tide".

[1] Boteler, p. 147.

73

King John's forces, "all unwarily" taken by the tide in the fords of the Wash, are rightly described as "Devoured by the unexpected *flood*" (5.7.64). Earlier, his ships reach France "upon the swelling *tide*" (2.1.74), "swelling" being an alternative word for "rising", as in "my uncontrolled tide . . . but swells the higher by this let" (*Lucrece* 645). There are other examples of "swell" applied to the rising tide, or to the rising volume of water in a river, "Cydnus swelled above the banks" (*Cymb.* 2.4.71).

The term "the swell" (*Ant. and Cleo.* 3.2.51) is used in the sense of high water until the eighteenth century, and never means, as it does now, low waves, cylindrical in shape, set up by wind that is past or at a distance.

As Prospero's spell begins to break, the returning consciousness and growing awareness of those in the charmed circle is likened to the rising of the tide:

> Their understanding
> Begins to swell, and the approaching tide
> Will shortly fill the reasonable shore,
> That now lies foul and muddy.   5.1.80

Achilles, selfcontained and making his will his law, is compared by Agamemnon with the tide.

> His pettish lunes, his ebbs, his flows, as if
> The passage and whole carriage of this action
> Rode on his tide.   *Troil. and Cres.* 2.3.137

THE STAND

The period at high or low water, during which no rise or fall can be detected, is known as the "stand". Shakespeare describes it accurately:

> 'Tis with my mind
> As with the tide swelled up unto his height,
> That makes a still-stand, running neither way: 2 *Hen. IV* 2.3.63

Or

> the swan's down feather,
> That stands upon the swell at full of tide
> And neither way inclines.   *Ant. and Cleo.* 3.2.50

In answering Olivia's question, "Of what personage and years is he?", Malvolio uses the figure of the stand:

> "'tis with him in standing water, between boy and man,"
> *T. Night* 1.5.168

and the conspirators in *The Tempest* also make use of it in their veiled words:

> "Well, I am standing water.—I'll teach you how to flow." 2.1.221

EDDIES

In tidal rivers, at certain stages of the tide, part of the stream may be deflected by some point of land, islet, projection or pier, and form eddies which may combine as a stream flowing in the opposite direction to that of the main stream:

> As through an arch the violent roaring tide
> Outruns the eye that doth behold his haste,
> Yet in the eddy boundeth in his pride
> Back to the strait that forced him on so fast;
> In rage sent out, recall'd in rage, being past: *Lucrece* 1667

Such is Shakespeare's dramatic but exact way of describing in verse what Mainwaring, in picturesque Jacobean prose, speaks of as "the running back of the water in some place contrary to the tide, and so falling into the tide again".[1]

WIND AND TIDE

When a strong tidal stream is flowing against the wind, a short steep sea is raised which can be dangerous to shipping and perilous to small craft. "A windward tide is when the tide runs against the sea and wind; then the sea breaks most and goes highest."[2] Shakespeare understands what takes place:

> Now sways it this way, like a mighty sea
> Forced by the tide to combat with the wind;
> Now sways it that way, like the selfsame sea
> Forced to retire by fury of the wind:
> Sometime the flood prevails, and then the wind. 3 *Hen. VI* 2.5.6

Even if wind and tide are going one way in tidal rivers, conditions as spectacular as they may be difficult can be set up if the wind is strong. The rush of waters between the arches of London Bridge, when the wind was with the tide, was a striking sight, and may be recalled in *Coriolanus*:

> Ne'er through an arch so hurried the blown tide,
> As the recomforted through the gates. 5.4.50

[1] Mainwaring, Vol. II, p. 143.   [2] Mainwaring, Vol. II, p. 244.

It had also impressed Frobisher who, during his third voyage, was reminded of it by a swift current in the area of the Queen's Foreland:

> "And truely it was wonderfull to heare and see the rushing and noise that the tides do make in this place with so violent a force . . . and the noyse of the streame no lesse to be heard afarre off, then the waterfall of London Bridge."[1]

While a strong favouring wind may enable a great ship to make headway against the tide:

> as rigour of tempestuous gusts
> Provokes the mightiest hulk against the tide,   1 *Hen. VI* 5.5.6

the efforts of water birds to do the same are in vain:

> I have seen a swan
> With bootless labour swim against the tide,
> And spend her strength with over-matching waves.   3 *Hen. VI* 1.4.20

And, in the days of sail, it was true to say, "It boots not to resist both wind and tide" 3 *Hen. VI* 4.3.59.

Of the shouts, calls and orders from the everyday world of a busy port, the most urgent are about the tide. "You'll lose the tide, if you tarry any longer" (*T.G. of V.* 2.3.34), "The tide is now;" (2.2.14), "Both wind and tide stays for this gentleman!" (*C. of E.* 4.1.46).

The horror of being cut off and engulfed by the tide is captured in *Titus Andronicus*:

> For now I stand as one upon a rock,
> Environ'd with a wilderness of sea;
> Who marks the waxing tide grow wave by wave,
> Expecting ever, when some envious surge
> Will in his brinish bowels swallow him.   3.1.93

The English soldiers on the eve of Agincourt think of themselves as faced with such a fate, "Even as men wracked upon a sand, that look to be washed off the next tide" (*Hen. V* 4.1.97). And it forms part of a choice of evils set before the followers of Henry VI:

> Tread on the sand; why, there you quickly sink,
> Bestride the rock; the tide will wash you off
> Or else you famish: that's a three-fold death.   3 *Hen. VI* 5.4.30

[1] *The Principal Navigations*, by Richard Hakluyt, Vol. VII (1904), p. 334.

In making Othello refer to:

> the Pontic sea,
> Whose icy current and compulsive course
> Ne'er feels retiring ebb, but keeps due on
> To the Propontic and the Hellespont: 3.3.454

Shakespeare is using floating knowledge about the Euxine that had come down from Pliny. "And the sea Pontus ever more floweth and runneth out into Propontis, but the sea never retireth backe againe within Pontus."[1] He avoids the terms "tide" and "stream" and uses "current" instead, for this covered a variety of the movements of the ocean. Many of these were imperfectly understood, and some not at all, though the problems they set were realised.

In the great lines which liken human life to voyaging, nautical wording falls into place naturally, and tide, flood, full sea and current are so wrought into the noble image and blended in the harmony of sound, that the exactness with which they are used passes all but unheeded.

> There is a *tide* in the affairs of men
> Which, taken at the flood, leads on to fortune;
> Omitted, all the *voyage* of their life
> Is *bound* in *shallows* and in miseries.
> On such a *full sea* are we now *afloat*,
> And we must *take the current* when it serves,
> Or lose our ventures.[2] *Julius Caesar* 4.3.216

The death of Falstaff is surrounded with pathos and a deep sense of the mystery of the threadlike life of man linked to forces that move the universe:

> a' parted even just between twelve and one,
> even at the turning o' the tide. *Hen. V* 2.3.11

It is an old belief, and still clung to round the sea coasts, that when life ebbs naturally, it is in this way. "Hereunto addeth *Aristotle* ... that no living creature dieth but in the refluxe and ebbe of the sea."[3]

---

[1] *The Historie of the World, commonly called the Naturall Historie of C. Plinius Secundus. Translated into English by Philemon Holland* (1601), 2 vols., Bk. 2, chap. 97, p. 43.
[2] All these terms are technically correct.
Pliny's *Historie of the World etc.*, translated by Philemon Holland, Vol. II, (1601), p. 98.

TRINITY HOUSE

The Trinity House of Deptford Strand was granted its first royal chapter on 20 May 1514, and this marked the refounding of a guild or fraternity of mariners empowered to make laws and ordinances "for the relief, increase, and augmentation of the shipping of this our realm of England".[1] Charters were also granted to similar corporations at Newcastle upon Tyne in 1536 and Kingston upon Hull in 1541.

The powers and responsibilities of Trinity House were further extended by the Act of 1565, "Concerning sea-marks and Mariners", which forbade the destruction of "beacons and marks of ancient time" and authorised Trinity House to maintain all that were necessary for the safety of ships, and also to set up more.

> "Divers ships with their goods and merchandizes . . . have by the lack of such marks of late years been miscarried, perished, and lost in the sea, to the great detriment and hurt of the commonweal, and the perishing of no small number of people."[2]

It is not surprising to find references in Shakespeare to marks and buoys and beacons, when his century saw the rise of Trinity House and the lessening of the dangers of grounding and shipwreck amid the shoals and sandbanks of the Thames through the efforts of its guild of pilots at Deptford. But, besides these practical matters, seamarks and beacons have associations of a wider kind, standing as they do for guidance and protection, safeguard and rescue. Indeed, one great aim of Trinity House, "to save and keep them, and the ships in their charge",[2] lends solemn impressiveness to the prayer of Coriolanus for his young son:

> The god of soldiers
> With the consent of supreme Jove, inform
> Thy thoughts with nobleness: that thou mayest prove
> To shame unvulnerable, and stick i' the wars
> Like a great sea-mark, standing every flaw,
> And saving those that eye thee! 5.3.70

[1] *Memoir on the Origin and Incorporation of the Trinity House of Deptford Strond*, by Joseph Cotton (1818), Appendix I., p. 163 [2] Ibid, p. 166.

To be as the great seamark, withstanding every violent gust, and saving those that look to it, is what he would have for

> This boy that cannot tell what he would have,
> But kneels and holds up hands for fellowship. 5.3.174

In Sonnet 116, which has more navigational terms than any other, the seamark is an emblem of constancy:

> an ever fixed mark
> That looks on tempests and is never shaken

And, in *Othello*, it stands for the utmost limit of the voyage of life:

> Here is my journey's end, here is my butt,
> And very sea-mark of my utmost sail. 5.2.265

Natural landmarks, such as tall trees and woods near the shore which enabled ships to take bearings, were known as beacons, as were pillars, towers of brick or stone, or posts and masts set up on the coasts for the direction of shipping by day. Later in Elizabeth's reign, however, the beacon was mostly a luminous mark to aid ships by night.

> See, noble Charles, the beacon of our friend,
> The burning torch in yonder turret stands. 1 *Hen. VI* 3.2.29
> Let not our ships and number of our men
> Be, like a beacon fired, t'amaze your eyes. *Per.* 1.4.87
>   "It illumineth the face, which as a beacon,
> gives warning to all the rest of this little
> kingdom, man." 2 *Hen. IV* 4.3.117

Lighthouses were not favoured till after 1600, because it was held that they might be of aid to an enemy or to pirates.

Buoys were of as great importance as beacons in coastal waters and, in *King Lear*, seen from the cliff top, is

> a buoy
> Almost too small for sight. *King Lear* 4.6.20

PILOTS

"Pilots are properly those who (upon coasts and shores unknown unto the Master) are employed for the conduction of ships into roads and harbours ... And this they perform by their being acquainted with the depths, heights, and the flowings of the tides ... and likewise by their knowledge of those kinds of sands as are moveable by the blowing of the winds."[1]

[1] Boteler, p. 25.

After the granting of the charter to Trinity House in 1514, the training and licensing of pilots came to be of increasing importance and different categories grew up. There were harbour pilots and coastal pilots. "A bare pilot serves only for the port he is hired for; but the coaster serves not only for such a place but for the whole coast."[1] And there were also pilots who could be borne for a whole voyage. By 1603, it was thought "no unthrifty providence, especially in ships of charge, to have one of them continually aboard for the prevention of all hazards". Moreover, it came to be held particularly desirable "that to all ships royal of his Majesty there be an allowance of a pilot to be aways aboard when they are to be abroad in any voyage, or at the least that one of the Master's Mates be known to be sufficiently traded that way; if not the Master himself."[2]

The pilot in *Othello* is of this sort. He is an ocean-going pilot, borne for the whole expedition, and:

> Of very expert and approved allowance.   2.1.48

The standing of such pilots was high and it is not unfitting that he should be sent ashore as Othello's official representative:

> These letters give, Iago, to the pilot;
> And by him do my duties to the Senate: 3.2.1

It is of the ocean-going pilot that Romeo is thinking when he says:

> I am no pilot: yet, wert thou as far
> As that vast shore washed with the farthest sea,
> I should adventure for such merchandise.   2.2.82

The pilot in the witches' chant in *Macbeth*, "Wracked as homeward he did come", is another of these ocean-going pilots, and might well be master and pilot in one, for this was not unusual in merchant ships.

The skilful pilot's charge is outlined in 3 *Henry VI*:

> For once allowed the skilful pilot's charge
> We will not from the helm . . .
> But keep our course, though the rough wind say no,
> From shelves and rocks that threaten us with wrack   5.4.20

and neglect of this is described in the form of a question, put for effect and answering itself:

> Yet lives our pilot still: is't meet that he
> Should leave the helm . . .
> Whiles in his moan, the ship splits on the rock,
> Which industry and courage might have saved?   5.4.6

[1] Monson, Vol. IV, pp. 30–31.   [2] Boteler, p. 28.

Romeo sees himself one such as this when he takes the fatal
potion:

> Thou desperate pilot, now at once run on
> The dashing rocks thy sea-sick weary bark! 5.3.117

Likenesses and similes make up the rest. Eyes and ears are:

> Two traded pilots 'twixt the dangerous shores
> Of will and judgement *Troil. and Cres.* 2.2.64

In *Lucrece*, "Desire my pilot is, beauty my prize." 279

The pilot and his hour glass are mentioned in *All's Well*
(2.1.168).

The appropriateness of these references throughout comes from
an understanding of "the requirable parts due to a good Pilot".[1]

---

[1] Boteler, p. 27.

G

DANGERS TO NAVIGATION

ROCKS AND SHOALS AND SANDBANKS

"Huge rocks, high winds, strong pirates, shelves and sands, The merchant fears... *Lucrece* 335

Dangers to shipping were of everyday concern and those that came from banks and shoals and shelves were very real to the citizens of London who not only heard and talked of them, but could see them as well.

Montgomery's treatise of 1570 dealt with the need for maintaining "in good state . . . the Thames or river of London, which dayly falleth to decay and ruine from the Brige down to Purphelet [Purfleet], wher the chanell is decayd in moste places fyve foot . . . besyde a number of Banckes and shelves, that have encreased and dayly doe encrease . . .".

The work of keeping the river navigable and "fitt for good shippes" had to be continuous, for otherwise there would have been "great hurt to the commonwealthe of that moste ancyent and famous citty",[1] fol. 16.

Mariners, merchants, adventurers all told of further dangers in the approaches to the coasts or out at sea. Manuals of navigation, sea cards and rutters gave warnings and directions, and the famous *Mariners Mirrour* (1588) had an important section on shoals, sands, flats and hidden rocks, including a set of symbols for buoys and beacons that showed where these lay.

The *Merchant of Venice* opens with talk of the hazards of seafaring. The merchant's pride in his "argosies with portly sail" must always be offset by fears for their safety and by uneasy thoughts of what has been risked:

.... but even now worth this,
And now worth nothing. 1.1.35

Anything he catches sight of may be enough to set his mind "tossing on the ocean", or to send him "Peering in maps for ports and piers and roads;"

[1] "A treatise cōcerning the nauie of England written in anno 1570 by In° Mountgomery with an addicion therto made by the saide author in an° 1588." British Museum, Add. MS. 20.042

I should not see the sandy hour-glass run.
But I should think of shallows and of flats;
                        Should I go to church.
And see the holy edifice of stone,
And not bethink me straight of dangerous rocks.   1.1.25

When Bassanio seeks to borrow on no better security than
Antonio's ventures at sea, Shylock at once reminds him:

> "But ships are but boards, sailors but men ... and then there is the
> peril of waters, winds, and rocks."   1.3.21

Dangers abound:

> "The scarfed bark puts from her native bay"

but, even if not overtaken by disaster,

> "How like the prodigal doth she return,
> With over-weathered ribs, and ragged sails,
> Lean, rent, and beggared."   2.6.15 ff.

A rumour of shipwreck itself is made convincing by its realism:

> "Antonio hath a ship of rich *lading wracked* on the narrow seas; the
> Goodwins, I think they call the place: a very dangerous *flat* and fatal,
> where the *carcasses* of many a *tall ship* lie buried."   3.1.3

Exact nautical and technical terms are used, and the description
of the area of danger is similar to what is given in sea cards and
manuals:

> "Goodwin is steepe and uneven, for at one casting of the
> lead you shall have 26 fathome, and at another cast of the lead
> you shall be fast upon the Sand."[1]

The Goodwins bring disaster to the Dauphin's supply ships in
King John:

> And your supply which you have wished so long
> Are cast away and sunk on Goodwin sands.   5.5.11–13

Through the centuries, they have been the cause of innumerable
wrecks, and still today, lightships, buoys, fog signals and even
guns give warning that they are near.

Bank, flat, sands, shelf, shoal are used precisely. A flat is an
extended sandbank or shallow. It can also mean the level fore-
shore or a low-lying tract over which the tide flows:

> half my power this night,
> Passing these flats, are taken by the tide.   *K. John* 5.6.40

Or:

> The ocean, overpeering of his list,
> Eats not the flats with more impetuous haste.   *Ham.* 4.5.100

[1] W. J. Blaeu, *The Light of Navigation* (1612), p. 27.

Caliban calls down on Prospero:

> All the infections that the sun sucks up
> From bogs, fens, flats.   *Temp.* 2.2.2

"Shoal and shallow are all one." When it is said that there is good shoaling, "it is meant that the water doth grow shallower by degrees ... nor sometimes deep, and sometimes suddenly a shoal, or bank".[1]

> upon this bank and shoal of time,[2]
> We'ld jump the life to come.   1.7.6

breaks from Macbeth as he struggles with his conscience and weighs time against eternity.

Wolsey, urging Cromwell to throw away ambition, thinks of deeps and shallows and shoals:

> Say, Wolsey, that once trod the ways of glory,
> And sounded all the depths and shoals of honour,
> Found thee a way, out of his wrack, to rise in.   *Hen. VIII* 3.2.436

A shelf is a bank of sand in the sea or in a river. Falstaff, after being thrown into the Thames, tells Bardolph:

> "I had been drown'd, but that the shore was shelvy and shallow—a death that I abhor:"   *Merry Wives* 3.5.15

The dangers of "shelves and rocks that threaten us with wrack" are recalled in 3 *Hen. VI* 5.4.23.

"Gall'd rocks and congregated sands" (*Oth.* 2.1.69), are dreaded almost equally. The rocks on which the vessel splits and the quicksands that draw it in are brought together in one of Queen Margaret's many powerful lines:

> "The splitting rocks cower'd in the sinking sands"   2 *Hen. VI* 3.2.97

"The ship splits on the rock" (3 *Hen. VI* 5.4.10), is "encountered by a mighty rock" (*C. of E.* 1.1.102), turns its stem "upon a dreadful rock" (2 *Hen. VI* 3.2.91). "The dashing rocks" await the "sea-sick weary bark" (*R. and J.* 5.3.118). Figuratively, Richard III is "a ragged, fatal rock" (3 *Hen. VI* 5.4.27), and Wolsey, in Norfolk's advice to Buckingham which comes too late, is "that rock That I advise your shunning" (*Hen. VIII* 1.1.113).

Engulfing quicksands, however, may be a means of defence:

> sands that will not bear your enemies' boats,
> But suck them up to th' topmast.   *Cymb.* 3.1.21

and even "merchant marring rocks"[3] may prove a bastion. An

---

[1] Mainwaring, Vol. II, p. 224.   [2] Emended reading.   [3] *M. of V.* 3.2.274.

enemy will find the western coasts of Britain "ribbed and paled in With rocks unscaleable" and his shipping "crackt . . . 'gainst our rocks". *Cymb.* 3.1.29–35.

Rocks become the emblem of what outlasts and withstands. Wolsey protests to the King that, in duty, he will be steadfast as "a rock against the chiding flood" (*Hen. VIII* 3.2.197), and Buckingham avers that he will make his vouch "as strong as shore of rock" (*Hen. VIII* 1.1.158).

SOUNDING

Sounding the great deeps could not have been attempted in Shakespeare's day, nor were the means to do it discovered till the nineteenth century. Soundings were taken when a ship had left the open ocean and had reached the hundred-fathom line which marks the outer edge of the Continental Shelf. Here the sea-bed drops down almost sheer for thousands of fathoms, "deeper than did ever plummet sound".[1] In some areas, this may occur a few hundred miles out to sea, but, off the coast of Spain and Portugal, the edge of the Shelf is only ten or twenty miles from the land. So when Rosalind, in *As You Like It*, says, "how many fathom deep I am in love! But it cannot be sounded", it is very apt that she should add, "my affection hath an unknown bottom, like the Bay of Portugal" (4.1.211).

Soundings were reckoned in fathoms, a fathom being six feet. It was also a measure for ropes, or the drop of a cliff "that looks so many fathoms to the sea" (*Ham.* 1.4.77), or for depths in the ground, "I'll break my staff, Bury it certain fathoms in the earth" (*Temp.* 5.1.55).

On "coming into soundings", that is, on reaching water of a hundred fathoms or less, the mariner had to look out for dangers from rocks, shoals and currents, and had to *try* the depth of water and *find* the nature of the ground for, "according to the depth and ground ... when we can see no land yet we know where we are".[2]

> "When ye be at Lxxx fadome ye shall finde small black sande and yee shalbe at the thwart of lezarde."[3]

The instruments used for taking soundings in deeper water were the deep-sea line, which Shakespeare calls the fathom line, and the deep-sea lead, a long plummet, which was attached to it.

In search of martial honour, Hotspur is prepared to

> dive into the bottom of the deep
> Where fathom line could never touch the ground.   1 *Hen. IV* 1.3.204

[1] *The Tempest* 5.1.56.
[2] Mainwaring, Vol. II, p. 140.   [3] Robert Copland, *The Rutter of the Sea* (1550), n.p., Biiii.

Here, the correct terms employed in sounding: "line", "touch", "ground", are kept to carefully.

In shoal water, on the other hand, that is in depths of less than twenty fathoms, the sounding lead and line, not the deep-sea lead and line, were used. These are not mentioned, but the lesser depths for which they were adapted find a place in Ariel's song "Full fathom five", and in the reference to Wolsey, "All the commons ... Wish him ten fathom deep" (*Hen. VIII* 2.1.51). In *King Lear*, Edgar's call, "Fathom and half, fathom and half!" (3.4.37), may have been that of inshore fishermen when taking soundings in shallow water, or of the Thames watermen working among the shoals.

The lower end of the plummet was "armed" with hard, white tallow. This ensured that mud or gravel would stick and that the plummet would "bring up the ground" to be inspected. The nature of the sea-bed varies. It may be of sand or gravel or ooze. Ooze is soft, muddy ground, and the "oozy bed", "the ooze and bottom of the sea", "the ooze of the salt deep",[1] is the only type that Shakespeare mentions:

> Therefore my son i' th' ooze is bedded; and
> I'll seek him deeper than e'er plummet sounded,
> And with him there lie mudded. 3.3.101

Ship, sounding line, sea-bed and haven are all brought together in the sorrowful words of Belarius:

> O melancholy,
> Who ever yet could sound thy bottom, find
> The ooze, to show what coast thy sluggish crare[2]
> Migh'st easil'est harbour in? *Cymb.* 4.2.203

It is in keeping with that blend of the practical and the imaginative which is strongly marked in his character. The skilled and active side is seen in his exact use of technical terms: *sound, bottom, find, ooze*, but to connect melancholy with un-plumbed deeps and a slow-moving attendant craft seeking an anchorage in suitable holding ground, belongs to a reflective and creative mind with that ability to perceive likenesses that goes with high endowment.

"Unsounded deeps" and all that "the profound seas hide in unknown fathoms",[3] fill the mind with an overwhelming sense

---

[1] *Temp.* 5.1.151; *Hen. V* 1.2.164; *Temp.* 1.2.252; *Per.* 3.1.61.   [2] Emended reading.
[3] *T.G. of V.* 3.2.81; *W.T.* 4.4.491.

of the unreachable, and no words of farewell could be more final, no words of abjuring more absolute than Prospero's as he takes leave of his art:

> And deeper than did ever plummet sound
> I'll drown my book.　5.1.56

NAVIGATIONAL INSTRUMENTS

George Best in his work *A Trve Discovrse*, written in 1578, re-
marked that the making of seacards, the use of the compass and
hour glass and of instruments for taking latitude and longitude
were so well known to every mariner "that he that hath bin
twice at Sea, is ashamed to come home, if he be not able to
render accompte of all these particularities".[1]

Of the more important, Shakespeare's knowledge is professional.
The card or seacard, mentioned in *Macbeth*:

> All the quarters that they know
> I' th' shipman's card,   1.3.17

was "a geographical description of coasts, with the true distances,
heights and courses, or winds laid down in it; not describing any
inland, which belongs to maps".[2] It was a kind of chart and is
twice referred to figuratively in *Hamlet*:

> "We must speak by the card or equivocation will undo us"   5.1.149

or later, with some play on words:

> "he is the card or calendar of gentry, for you shall find in him the
> continent of what parts a gentleman would see."   5.2.114

In Shakespeare, *card* does not mean the graduated compass card
or "fly", because it did not come to have this sense till after his
day.

The compass is "that movable instrument with a fly whereon
are described the 32 points or winds, by which we direct or steer
our courses at sea".[3] A point is eleven-and-a-quarter degrees,
and the thirty-two points make up a full circle. Much was being
written about the compass in the later sixteenth century, and
Archdeacon William Barlow's work, *The Navigator's Supply* (1597),
led to some far-reaching improvements in it.

> "I think if all our wits were to issue out of one skull, they would fly
> east, west, north, south, and their consent of one direct way should be
> at once to all the points of the compass."   *Coriolanus* 2.3.26

[1] Preface.   [2] Mainwaring, Vol. II, p. 117.
[3] Mainwaring, Vol. II, p. 129.

This, in a great age of navigation, is a topical way of describing mass confusion, and the Roman citizen is made to speak like an Elizabethan.

There are two examples of how the mariner's compass is read; a straightforward reading of an intermediate point in *Hamlet*: "I am but mad north-northwest" (2.2.396), and another in *Love's Labour's Lost* which is more complicated and shows Armado's liking for extreme precision: "It standeth north-northeast and by east" (1.1.248). It was the seaman's habit to insert 'and' in this way when reading off half and quarter points, perhaps because the words could be sung out more easily and there was less risk of mishearing.

DIALS

Pocket dials were of great aid to seafarers and to travellers. Touchstone in the forest of Arden "drew a dial from his poke" and Jaques "did laugh sans intermission An hour by his dial". They were constructed to tell time in much the same way as a sundial:

> Thou by thy dial's shady stealth mayest know
> Time's thievish progress to eternity   *Sonnet 77*

and also to give information about sunrise, sunset and the tides that was later supplied by pocket almanacs.

> To carve out dials quaintly point by point
> Thereby to see the minutes how they run   3 *Hen. VI* 2.5.24

was an art. "Many lines close in the dial's centre" (*Hen. V* 1.2.210), and skilled craftsmanship was required to engrave them and "those bars which stop the hourly dial" (*Lucrece* 327).

Two early dials of historic interest have survived. One, said to have belonged to Drake and dated 1569, is preserved in the National Maritime Museum, and another dated 1593 which belonged to Essex is in the British Museum. Its nocturnal is of fine workmanship and is designed for use with the Guards of Ursa Minor.[1]

Dials were expensive, unlike annual almanacs which, costing little, were widely used ashore and also at sea. The almanac contained a calendar with a section giving the phases of the moon: "A calendar, a calendar! look in the almanac, find out moonshine,

---

[1] See Stars, p. 93.

find out moonshine" (*M.N.D.* 3.1.55). Another section had to do with the planets and stars. The remark "Saturn and Venus this year in conjunction! what says the almanac to that?" (2 *Henry IV* 2.4.262), is burlesque, for such a conjunction never takes place. A popular, but often unsettling, addition to the almanac was the Prognostication, and Edmund in *King Lear* seems to have been consulting one: "I am thinking, brother, of a prediction I read this other day, what should follow these eclipses" (1.2.147).

The glass or sand glass was indispensable to the mariner:

> Or four and twenty times the pilot's glass
> Hath told the thievish minutes how they pass. *All's Well*, 2.1.168

In Shakespeare's day, it was an hour glass, and his references are to the hour glass only:

> Ere the glass that now begins to run
> Finish the process of his sandy hour. 1 *Hen. VI* 4.2.35

In *The Tempest*, "at least two glasses" (1.2.240) and "three glasses since" (5.1.223) indicate the passing of two and three hours. Other examples occur in the *Merchant of Venice*, "I should not see the sandy hour-glass run" (1.1.25), in *The Winter's Tale* (1.2.306, 4.1.16) and in *Henry V* (1 Prol. 31). Later, the halfhour glass became the more usual means of measuring time.

GLOBES AND MAPS

With Emery Molyneux, the making of globes reached a degree of perfection that made Robert Hues of Oxford say, "There seems not to be anything that may be added to them".

Hues, a good classical scholar who decided to devote himself to mathematics and geography, made at least two voyages for practical experience, one being to the southern hemisphere with Cavendish in 1591–92, and he then brought out an important treatise on globes and their uses.[1]

"There are two kinds of Instruments by which Artificers have conceived that the figure of this so beautifull and various fabricke of the whole Universe might most aptly be expressed, and as it were at once presented to the view. The one exhibiting this Idea in a round solid is called a Globe or Sphaere. The

[1] *Tractatus de Globis et Eorum Usu*, by Robert Hues (1594), 8vo. It was edited by Clements R. Markham for the Hakluyt Society in 1889.

other, expressing the same in a Plaine, they tearme a Planis-
phaere, or Map."[1]

Hues, in discussing the rival merits of globes and maps, gave
preference to globes, contending that besides beauty and grace
of form, they were best suited to the understanding and fancy
because they gave a natural, fitting and proper image of things.

Globes are referred to only twice in Shakespeare, but this
happens to be in contexts that do not offer any chance of
mentioning the elegance of their workmanship.[2]

Edward Wright's famous *Map of the World* appeared in 1600.
It was based on Mercator's idea of a projection which would
represent rhumb lines as straight lines, but Mercator had been
unable to demonstrate how the groundwork should be laid down.
This, Wright was the first to do, and he justly claimed "the way
how this should be done I learned neither of Mercator nor of
any one else".[3] He solved the problem of representing the earth's
curved surface upon a plane surface in such a way that courses and
distances could be accurately plotted by using a ruler and pro-
tractor, and this was of great advantage to navigators.

The interest created by the map can be seen in Shakespeare's
two references to it in *Twelfth Night*, one direct and the other
indirect:

> "he does smile his face into more lines than is in the new map,
> with the augmentation of the Indies:"   3.2.82

Northern Novaya Zemlya, discovered by the Dutchman
Barents in 1596, and his winter quarters there, "Het behouden
huys", were recorded on the northern portion of the map, and this
section soon appeared as a separate publication because of a demand for it.[4] These facts, incidental as they may be, seem to
lie behind Fabian's remark to Sir Andrew:

> "you are now sailed into the north of my lady's opinion; where you
> will hang like an icicle on a Dutchman's beard."   3.2.25

[1] Markham's edition, p. 5.   [2] *C. of E.* 3.2.116; 2 *Hen. IV* 2.4.309.
[3] *Errors* (1599), Preface, p. x.
[4] The Voyages and Works of John Davis *The Navigator*, edited by Albert H. Markham,
Hakluyt Society (1880), pp. lxxxv–xciii.

SAILING BY THE STAR

> These earthly godfathers of heaven's lights,
> That give a name to every fixed star,
> Have no more profit of their shining nights
> Than those that walk and wot not what they are. *L.L.L.* 1.1.84

While this may be true of the astronomer or wayfarer, it is not of the mariner, for certain stars or groups of stars enable him to find his direction by night. "What if the Sun do not shine at noon, nor perhaps all . . . day? You must tarry untill night that some starre appeare, which you perfectly know . . ."[1]

Of these the most important is the Pole star, known also as the Lodestar,[2] the Cynosure, the North star, the Northern star or simply the Star:

> Well, an' you be not turned Turk, there's no more sailing by the Star. *M. Ado.* 3.4.51

It has been the age-long safeguard of sailors, because lying as it does within one-and-a-half degrees of the line of the earth's axis, it always indicates, more or less, the direction of true north.

> I am constant as the northern star,
> Of whose true-fixed and resting quality
> There is no fellow in the firmament. *Julius Caesar* 3.1.60

The Pole star is part of the constellation Ursa Minor or the Little Bear and its position can be found from other nearby stars which serve as pointers. These are the Guards in Ursa Minor (Kochab and Y) and the two end stars (Dubhe and Merak) of Ursa Major, the Great Bear, also named the Plough. The Guards, being brighter, are often visible when the other stars of the Little Bear, including Polaris, are obscured.

> The wind-shaked surge, with high and monstrous mane,
> Seems to cast water on the burning bear,
> And quench the guards of the ever-fixed pole: *Oth.* 2.1.12

When a navigator spoke of the Guards he meant the Guards of Ursa Minor only, because he used them in making calculations. But, as the pointers of Ursa Major were sometimes called Guards in Shakespeare's day, either could be meant in this passage.

[1] Thomas Blundeville, *M. Blundevile His Exercises* (6th edition).   [2] Figuratively in *M.N.D.* 1.1.183; *Lucr.* 178

93

In *Sonnet 116*, the lines:

> It is the star to every wandering bark,
> Whose worth's unknown, although his height be taken

are a reminder that the Pole star enabled the navigator to determine his latitude or "height" as well as to check his course. He did this by noting from the position of the Guards whether the Pole star was above, below or to one side of the celestial pole. He then applied a correction, according to the Rule of the North Star, which allowed for the effect of the rotation of the Pole star about the celestial pole. This gave the true elevation of the pole above the horizon in degrees, and this was also his latitude.

The old astronomy of Ptolemy lingers in Shakespeare but the growing influence of the new theories of Copernicus is also seen. According to Ptolemy's system, the earth was a fixed centre.[1] Round it sun, moon, planets and stars revolved, and they moved in separate spheres: "the star moves not but in his sphere" (*Ham.* 4.7.15); "Two stars keep not their motion in one sphere" (1 *Hen. IV* 5.4.65).[2] Confusion and disaster were believed to follow, should the planets "to disorder wander" (*Troil. and Cres.* 1.3.94). The spheres were thought of as having a common centre, one enclosing another and their motion made "the music of the spheres" (*Per.* 5.1.231). In Cleopatra's vision of Antony, his voice "was propertied As all the tuned spheres" (5.2.84).[3]

The planets were known as the "wandering stars" (*Ham.* 5.1.259), to distinguish them from the "fixed stars" (*R. II* 2.4.9) which were observed to keep the same situation and distance from one another. Being in the eighth sphere or the firmament, the fixed stars, it was held, were not subject to change or corruption and this gives extreme edge to Benedick's remark about the effect of Beatrice's caustic tongue, "she would infect to the north star" (*M. Ado*, 2.1.232).

But on the new theories depended the solution of a problem connected with the motion of the planet Mars that Shakespeare took note of as early as 1 *Henry VI*:

> Mars his true moving, even as in the heavens,
> So in the earth, to this day is not known.   1.2.1

This was not finally explained until Kepler's investigations of the orbit of Mars were published in *De Motibus Stellae Martis*, 1609.

---

[1] *Troil. and Cres.* 1.3.85; *Ham.* 2.2.159.   [2] Also, *Ant and Cleo.* 2.7.16; *Ham.* 1.5.17.   [3] Also
A.Y.L. 2.7.6; *T.N.* 3.1.111.

Time could be reckoned from the position of the stars:

> I cannot, by the progress of the stars,
> Give guess how near to day   *Julius Caesar*, 2.1.2

says Brutus when he is much preoccupied, but the Carrier in
1 *Henry IV* has no such difficulty.

> "Heigh ho! An't be not four by the day I'll be hanged; Charles'
> Wain is over the new chimney"   2.1.1

The name was an everyday one for the Plough or Great Bear,
for the seven stars were thought to resemble a four-wheeled
wagon drawn by three horses.

Those who wish to use the day sky as a dial must keep in mind
that, in the northern hemisphere, the sun rises south of east in
midwinter and sets south of west. Thereafter, it rises and sets
farther and farther northwards until, by midsummer, it takes a
great sweep circling from approximately north-east, southwards
and westwards, to the north-west where it sets.

Casca, in putting his hearers right about the apparent direction
of sunrise, is really correcting the mistaken general idea that the
sun rises due east and sets due west all the year round, when it
does so only at the equinoxes on 21 March and 21 September.

Decius. Here lies the east: doth not the day break here?
Casca. No.
Cinna. O, pardon, sir, it doth; and yon grey lines
        That fret the clouds are messengers of day.
Casca. You shall confess that you are both deceived,
        Here, as I point my sword, the sun arises;
        Which is a great way growing on the south,
        Weighing the youthful season of the year.
        Some two months hence, up higher toward the north
        He first presents his fire; and the high east
        Stands, as the Capitol, directly here.   2.1.101 ff.

A tense point in the drama has been reached. The leaders of the
conspiracy talk apart, and the others fill in the interval with this
practical scientific discussion which takes their minds off the
desperate business they have in hand.

Besides what is of navigational and scientific interest, there are
many references to the stars as points of light in the night sky:
"bright, shining, twinkling;" or to their imagined connection
with human destiny: "auspicious, lucky, good, homely, happy,

or malignant, illboding and thwarting." Such superstitions are
looked at realistically by Cassius:

> Men at some time are masters of their fates:
> The fault, dear Brutus, is not in our stars,
> But in ourselves, that we are underlings. 1.2.137

And notions of the starred, star-crossed and of starblasting are
dismissed with mockery by Edmund in *King Lear*:

> "This is the excellent foppery of the world, that when we are sick in
> fortune, often the surfeit of our own behaviour, we make guilty of our
> disasters the sun, the moon, and stars; as if we were villains on neces-
> sity, fools by heavenly compulsion, knaves, thieves and treachers by
> spherical predominance." 1.2.132

TYPES OF SHIP

Many types of ship and sailing craft are referred to in the plays, often when there is no mention of them in the story or source that Shakespeare is adapting. The differences between them are clearly understood. Warships and merchant ships are carefully distinguished, there is no uncertainty and there is never any confusion.

WARSHIPS

Warships are given the general or collective name either of "man of war"—"leave you not a man of war unsearched" (*Tit. And.* 4.3.22); or "tall ship", a very English name, which includes armed merchantmen. Bolingbroke and his followers make for England "with eight tall ships", the prayer for Othello's safety is that he may "bless the bay with his tall ship", a "tall anchoring bark" completes the vista from the cliff in *King Lear*, and, on the Goodwins, "the carcasses of many a tall ship lie buried".[1]

Of the various kinds of warship, the galley was, from classical times, the main fighting ship of the Mediterranean. In *Antony and Cleopatra*, references are naturally to galleys, and the war at sea between the Venetians and Turks in *Othello* is introduced with reports of fleets of galleys. Antonio, in *Twelfth Night*, did some service "once in a sea fight 'gainst the Count his galleys", thus making it a typical Mediterranean engagement; and a fleet in the *Taming of the Shrew* includes "twelve tight galleys". Though unsuitable for northern waters, galleys came to be of interest in England between 1599 and 1602 when two squadrons were brought through the Straits of Gibraltar and up the Channel to Flanders, and it was suggested that a similar English force should be built to meet any threats of this sort. There was opposition, because it was held that "the proper use of galleys is against galleys in the Mediterranean sea that is subject to calms",[2] and the plan was given up.

[1] *R. II* 2.1.286; *Oth.* 2.1.79; *K. Lear* 4.6.18; *M. of V.* 3.1.6.   [2] Monson, Vol. IV, pp. 99–110.

The mention of two galliasses in the *Taming of the Shrew* is of some significance, for, after the defeat of the Armada, pleas were made for building them in English shipyards. In the "Addition" (1588) to his "Treatise" of 1570 on the navy,[1] John Montgomery argued that these vessels, being built to sail and to row, had an advantage over others, and he pointed out that four great galliasses of seven or eight hundred tons and well appointed with brass ordnance had come with the Spaniards in 1588. The matter was taken up and proposals put forward. The new ships, it was held, could be manned by recruiting the Thames bargemen, wherrymen, ferrymen, scullers and fishers, but after some debate, the scheme came to nothing.

In this way, lines that to a later age might seem to be merely high-sounding and rhetorical:

> my father hath no less
> Than three great argosies, besides two galliasses,
> And twelve tight galleys   *T. of S.* 2.1.370

were, for Shakespeare's hearers, connected with affairs and discussions of the day.

Smallest of all, but still a fighting ship, was the Pinnace, a light, square-rigged vessel of forty to a hundred tons, rarely more. It had auxiliary oars and carried guns. The Lieutenant in 2 *Henry VI* is captain of a pinnace,[2] and Falstaff in the *Merry Wives of Windsor*, speaks as if he had the same command.[3]

SHIP'S BOATS

Shakespeare also introduces boats belonging to warships, once again showing knowledge of what they are and of how they are employed. The Long-boat "the largest and the strongest of all such boats as are to be hoised into a ship",[4] carried heavy goods or conveyed members of a ship's company to and from shore. It is used in this way in 2 *Henry VI*, when the Lieutenant and others go ashore from the pinnace with their prisoners.

The Cock boat, described as "over-tender sided, and too small to be made use of in any service when a ship is abroad at sea",[5] is referred to only once and, fittingly, it is lying off a warship in an anchorage. Seen from the height of Dover Cliff, the tall anchoring bark seems diminished to the size of her

---

[1] See p. 82, note 1.   [2] See p. 4.   [3] See p. 69.
[4] Boteler, p. 195.   [5] Boteler, p. 197.

cock boat, and the cock boat appears no bigger than a buoy
(*King Lear* 4.6.20).

Barges "serve rather for bravery and state and ease (as to
carry the Admiral and prime Captains) than for any other
important service".[1] They were ornamental and often luxuriously
furnished, as in *Henry VIII*:

> Prepare there;
> The duke is coming; see the barge be ready,
> And fit it with such furniture as suits
> The greatness of his person.   2.1.98

Or:

> A noble troop of strangers,
> For so they seem: th' have left their barge and landed;
> And hither make, as great ambassadors
> From foreign princes.   1.4.53

Barges are rightly used for official visits in the harbour scene
in *Pericles*.[2] In the description of Cleopatra's barge, Shakespeare
gives a poetic rendering of Plutarch's account of the Queen of
Egypt's triumphant state, and his aim is to bring to life the
magnificence and luxury of the Orient.

> The barge she sat in, like a burnish'd throne,
> Burned on the water: the poop was beaten gold,
> Purple the sails, and so perfumed that
> The winds were love-sick with them; the oars were silver.   2.2.195

MERCHANT VESSELS

The Argosy was the stateliest of all merchant ships and, under
full canvas, was a splendid sight. This is pictured vividly and with
some grandeur in the *Merchant of Venice*.

> argosies with portly sail
> Like signiors and rich burghers on the flood,
> Or, as it were, the pageants of the sea.   1.1.9

As early as 3 *Henry VI*, the regal argosy had appealed to Shakespeare's imagination, and the domineering consort of "calm
Henry" is spoken of as driving him "though he were a king"

> As doth a sail, filled with a fretting gust
> Command an argosy to stem the waves.   2.6.36

Other references to the argosy are brief and occur in the *Taming
of the Shrew* 2.1.367, 369, 371; and in the *Merchant of Venice*
1.3.18, 3.1.105, 5.1.276.

---

[1] Boteler, p. 196.   [2] See pp. 20–21.

The Carrack or Carack was a large, armed merchantman usually of Spain or Portugal. To capture one on the high seas was the hope of Elizabethan adventurers. The most famous of such prizes was the *Madre de Dios* which was brought into Dartmouth in 1592, and proved a treasurehouse and warehouse in one.

Othello's good fortune in winning Desdemona provokes Iago to say, grudgingly and cynically:

> Faith, he tonight hath boarded a land carrack:
> If it prove lawful prize, he's made for ever.   1.2.50

Dromio's mock description of Nell in the *Comedy of Errors*, with its references to America, the Indies and Spain, includes, in a topical way, "whole armadoes of carracks to be ballast at her nose" (3.2.135).

Collectively, warships and armed merchantmen formed an Armada or Armado. In *King John*, "A whole armado of convicted sail Is scattered" (3.4.2). The word fell into disuse in the seventeenth century.

Hulk, though now applied to old and dismasted ships unfit for further seagoing, was, in Elizabethan days, the name given to the large merchantman of the northern nations. It was cumbersome and unseaworthy. Its carrying capacity and unwieldiness are chiefly in mind when it is said of Falstaff "you have not seen a hulk better stuffed in the hold" (2 *Hen. IV* 2.4.70). Its size gives point to the simile:

> And like as rigour of tempestuous gusts
> Provokes the mightiest hulk against the tide,   1 *Hen. VI* 5.5.5

while its slow motion and deep draught are taken note of in:

> Light boats sail swift, though greater hulks draw deep.
> *Troil. and Cres.* 2.3.263

These references, together, provide a concise description of the hulk. Shakespeare introduces all of them independently and unprompted by a source.

SMALL CRAFT

The "Buss" should not be overlooked. It was a two-masted or three-masted vessel much used for fishing in the sixteenth and seventeenth centuries. From time to time, the Queen and her

Council were petitioned to encourage the building of busses and pinks so that the national wealth might be increased.

In *The Tempest*, Prospero tells how Miranda and he were set adrift in:

> A rotten carcass of a butt, not rigg'd,
> Nor tackle, sail nor mast; 1.2.146

The reading "butt" is disputed and "boat" has been suggested instead. It is certainly strange to expect a "butt" to be rigged with tackle, sail and mast; some boats would not be. The passage is otherwise technically accurate. Shakespeare has even used "carcass" which is the shipwright's term for the skeleton of a vessel. As the buss was a wellknown craft at the time and also of some importance, there may be something to be said for reading "buss" instead of "butt".

The Pink, a fast sailing craft used for various purposes including fishing, is referred to aptly in the *Merry Wives of Windsor*.[1]

Cockle is a name for a variety of cock boat, but the lines:

> Thus time we waste, and long leagues make short;
> Sail seas in cockles, have and wish but for 't; *Per.* 4.4.1

occur in a context where the miraculous and impossible are being stressed, and the allusion may be to the folk belief that witches were able to sail on stormy seas in cockles or mussel shells.

Crare or crayer, a small trading vessel, is found in an emended line in Cymbeline, "Thy sluggish crare"[2] (4.2.205).

Gondola, the long narrow craft, with prow and stern tapering to a point, used chiefly on the canals of Venice, comes into the *Merchant of Venice* as might be expected. Jessica and Lorenzo are seen in one and, in *Othello*, Desdemona steals from her father's house attended by a gondolier. Rosalind's remark in *As You Like It*, "to have swum in a gondola", means to have been to Venice.[3]

The Hoy was useful as a tender for warships and large vessels. It did not have cross sails or yards but, according to Boteler, "sails cut into the form of mizen sails",[4] and it was thus able to sail much nearer to the wind than any vessel with cross yards could do. In the *Comedy of Errors*, where so much turns out to be the opposite of what was intended, the names of vessels are no

[1] See p. 70.   [2] See p. 87.
[3] *M. of. V.* 2.8.8; *Oth.* 1.1.126; *A.Y.L.* 4.1.38.   [4] Boteler, p. 197.

exception. The hoy, a craft designed to be fast sailing, is called "Delay".

> "I brought you word an hour since, that the bark Expedition put forth tonight: and then were you hindered by the sergeant, to tarry for the hoy Delay."   4.3.40

The names boat and ship should not be used loosely as if they were interchangeable. A boat, in the strict sense, is an open vessel as distinct from a ship. The difference is brought out in the account of "taking to the boats" in the *Comedy of Errors*:[1]

> The sailors sought for safety by our *boat*,
> And left the *ship*, then sinking ripe, to us.   1.1.77

It was the main means of rescue in shipwreck, but there could be drawbacks and dangers. Talbot finds it "too much folly"

> To hazard all our lives in one small boat!   1 *Hen. VI.* 4.6.33

In *Twelfth Night*, the shipwrecked cling to "a driving boat" (1.2.11). Boats are mostly used in plying from ship to shore:

> Richmond, in Dorsetshire, sent out a boat
> Unto the shore,   *R. III* 4.4.524

The light build of boats which makes them unable to live in rough seas is taken by Nestor as an example of the difference between "valour's show and valour's worth" in the storms of fortune:

> the sea being smooth,
> How many shallow bauble boats dare sail
> Upon her patient breast, making their way
> With those of nobler bulk!
> But let the ruffian Boreas once enrage
> The gentle Thetis, and anon behold
> The strong-ribbed bark through liquid mountains cut,
> Bounding between the two moist elements
> Like Perseus' horse; where's then the saucy boat
> Whose weak untimbered sides but even now
> Co-rivalled greatness?—either to harbour fled,
> Or made a toast for Neptune.   *Troil. and Cres.* 1.3.34 ff.

Boat may be used as a term of contempt for ship as when the Queen in *Cymbeline* speaks of "your enemies' boats" (3.1.22). Only once does it occur in the loose, general sense of vessel, where the stormbeaten ship in *Pericles* is "our dancing boat" (3.1.13).

Bark is a poetic variant for a vessel and does not mean, as later, a barque or three-masted ship.

[1] Also *Sonnet 80*.

ANCHORS AND CABLES

'What an Anchor is and wherefore it is, is as generally known as the ship itself."[1]

Without the anchor, fashioned of shank, ring, arms, flukes, bill and stock, a ship could not be secured to the sea-bottom and prevented from drifting.

Anchor work has its own set of terms. "If her anchors hold fast, and come not home (as the seaphrase is) she is said to ride."[2] Shakespeare uses these and others:

> You had much ado to make his *anchor hold*:
> When you *cast out*, it still *came home*.   *W. Tale*, 1.2.213

A ship rides "whenas her anchors do hold her fast so as that she doth not drive away with the tide or wind".[3]

> Be anchored in the bay where all men ride.   *Sonnet 137*

A ship that has come to anchor is said to be "at anchor" (*Per.* 5; *Chor.* 16). When casting anchor, it is said to "anchor". The pinnace in 2 *Henry VI* (4.1.9) "anchors in the Downs".

"Anchorage" meant a ship's set of anchors as well as a roadstead or place to anchor in, and to heave them up in preparation for sailing is "to weigh":

> Lo, as the bark that hath discharged her fraught
> Returns with precious lading to the bay
> From whence at first she weighed her anchorage,   *Tit. And.* 1.1.71

Staunch friends are likened to anchors (3 *Hen. VI* 5.4.16) and steadfast attachments to anchoring: "Posthumus anchors upon Imogen" (*Cymb.* 5.5.394). "The holding anchor lost," is how Queen Margaret describes the desperate state of her fortunes (3 *Hen. VI* 5.4.4). All anchors are for holding a ship, but what is meant here is the sheet anchor, "which is the biggest, and that which the seamen call their last hope, and is never used but in great extremity . . . this is the true *Anchora Spei*, for this is their last refuge".[4]

[1] Boteler, p. 187.   [2] Boteler, pp. 96–97.
[3] Mainwaring, Vol. II, p. 209.   [4] Mainwaring, Vol. II, p. 89.

CABLES

"A Cable is a three-strand rope intended to be sufficient for a ship to ride by at anchor, for otherwise it is counted but a hawser, for a great ship's hawser will make a small ship's cable."[1] The cable is made fast or "bent" to the anchor.

A way of putting to sea quickly in an emergency was to cut the hempen cable and leave the anchor on the bottom. This was known as "cut and run", and it is what Menas proposes to do in Pompey's galley:

> let me cut the cable;
> And, when we are put off, fall to their throats:
> *Ant. and Cleo.* 2.7.71

The Spaniards had done this in panic as they lay at anchor in Calais Roads. In the darkness, English fire ships were mistaken for powder ships or mine ships from which Spain had suffered in the Scheldt at the siege of Antwerp, "whereupon, crying out: The fire of Antwerp,—that forest of ships and vast galleons, tumultuously cutting their cables in their hawses, ran away in a shameful confusion by our northern seas".[2]

Sometimes the cable would part, "The cable broke" (3 *Hen. VI* 5.4.4), always a serious mishap.

Iago, who uses sea terms readily, professes to be knit "with cables of perdurable toughness" to Roderigo's "deserving" (1.3.343), and warns Othello that Brabantio will act against him as far as the law "Will give him cable" (1.2.17).

When the storm is at its height, Gonzalo thinks longingly of the security of a ship riding at anchor by her cable. For them, anchoring is impossible, because they must sail past the island or run aground. Their best hope of escaping shipwreck seems to lie in his belief that the boatswain "will be hanged yet, Though every drop of water swear against it", so he entreats:

> "Stand fast, good Fate, to his hanging: make the rope of his destiny our cable, for our own doth little advantage." *Temp.* 1.1.30 ff.

[1] Mainwaring, Vol. II, p. 113.   [2] Boteler, pp. 312-13.

THE PARTS OF A SHIP

In *The Tempest*, several of the main parts of a ship are named briefly and in order—beak, waist, deck, cabin, topmast, yards—and many more are referred to in other plays.

The Beak or Beakhead is fastened to the stem and supported with a knee, "and it is indeed the becoming part and the main grace and beauty of a ship".[1]

A cabin is a room in a ship, a private apartment for living in: "make yourself ready in your cabin," "keep your cabins," "To cabin" (*Temp.* 1.1.28, 15, 18). "Upon from my cabin," says Hamlet, "in the dark Groped I," then lapses into the landsman's term as he goes on with his story, "and in fine withdrew To mine own *room* again" (5.2.12). "Room" in royal naval ships was, and is, applied to compartments for stores: the powder room, the spirit room, the bread room, the sail room. Instead of leaving Menas to go ashore, Enobarbus hospitably says, "No, to my cabin" (2.7.129), and Clarence tells how his brother Gloster "from my cabin tempted me to walk" (*R. III* 1.4.12).

Decks are the planked "floors" of a ship extending from side to side. There is nothing in Shakespeare's use of the word itself that needs explanation and there are only a few examples of it, but these are important because of the sea phrases in which they occur. To remain on deck, as Posthumus does till land is lost to sight, is to "*keep* the deck" (*Cymb.* 1.4.11). Pericles "endured a sea That almost *burst* the deck" (4.1.57). It would be incorrect to use "split". "*Above* deck", as opposed to "below deck" or "between decks", comes into the *Merry Wives of Windsor*.[2]

Hatches are "those loose parts, or as it were doors, of the deck which are in the midship before the mainmast, that we open to let down things into the hold".[3] This early seventeenth century definition covers Shakespeare's use of the term. After the storm in *The Tempest*, the mariners are left "all under hatches stowed" (1.2.230). They are later reported asleep "Under the hatches" (5.1.99) and wake up to find themselves, they know not how,

---

[1] Boteler, p. 75. [2] See p. 69. [3] Mainwaring, Vol. II, p. 160.

"all clapped[1] under hatches" (5.1.231). Margaret, in 2 *Henry VI*, "stood upon the hatches in the storm" (3.2.103), a vantage point amidships. Clarence paces "Upon the giddy footing of the hatches" (*R. III* 1.4.17). There is no need to explain these last two references by going back to the ship construction of an earlier period when hatches meant the movable planking that formed the deck, and when vessels might be without bulwarks in the waist. Shakespeare is not following a chronicle or any source here and he preferred what was familiar to his own age.

The Hold is the whole interior cavity of a ship, or all that part between the bottom timbers and the lowest deck. Hold occurs only once. Falstaff is likened to a hulk "stuffed in the hold" (2 *Hen. IV* 2.4.62). To say "stowed" would not be appropriate because, when used precisely, *stow* means to put in the hold in proper order. Stow is not applied to "small things, as to a chest or the like",[2] so in *Pericles* the sailor says, simply but correctly, "Sir, we have a chest *beneath* the hatches" (3.1.70), omitting "stowed". There is some play on "stuff". Falstaff is "stuffed" for "there's a whole merchant's venture of Bordeaux stuff in him". Wine is meant, but to call it by a name that has other associations is hardly an accident. *Stuff* was a sea term for a mixed mass of tallow, sulphur and resin: or tar, whale oil and broken glass used to smear or "pay" the sides or bottom of a ship to preserve it from water or weather. A suggestion of double meaning would carry with it a delicate tribute to Falstaff, but it would not be out of keeping with Mrs. Ford's compliment to him in the *Merry Wives of Windsor*:

> "What tempest, I trow, threw this whale, with so many tuns of oil in his belly ashore at Windsor?"   2.1.57

The Hull is the main body of a ship. From it comes "to hull", which is to take in sails, usually in stress of weather, so that nothing but masts, yards and rigging are abroad, and to lash the helm a-lee. Henry VIII, speaking of his "many mazed considerings" about the succession and the lawfulness of his marriage, concludes:

> Thus hulling in
> The wild sea of my conscience, I did steer
> Toward this remedy.   2.4.199

In *Twelfth Night*, when Maria asks, "Will you hoist sail, sir?", Viola replies, "I am to hull here a little longer" (1.5.207),

---

[1] In the general sense of "secured".   [2] Mainwaring, Vol. II, p. 238.

which is a suitable answer, for she is like a ship that has taken all sails in, and is neither riding securely at anchor nor yet drifting. Richmond's "puissant navy" lies hulling off the western coast:

> And there they hull, expecting but the aid
> Of Buckingham to welcome them ashore. *R. III* 4.4.438

HELM AND RUDDER

The Helm is a piece of timber or a bar put into the rudder of a ship to guide or steer her. "At the helm a seeming mermaid steers" Cleopatra's barge. Suffolk, in a figure, promises the ambitious Margaret, "And you yourself shall steer the happy helm" (2 *Hen. VI*, 1.3.103).[1] The phrase "steer the helm" has been questioned, but Shakespeare is not in error. Mainwaring uses it: "In smaller ships, . . . they use to put a whip to the other end of the helm and so steer and govern the helm by that."[2]

The order to the helmsman "bear up" means to put the helm up to windward, "which when you do the ship falls from the wind and goes down the wind".[3] This enabled it to bear down on an enemy. Stephano calls out accurate directions for an assault of this kind in the midst of his talk about refilling their bottle from a butt of wine: "therefore bear up, and board 'em" (*Temp*. 3.2.2). A fleet is reported "bearing up to Cyprus" in *Othello* (1.3.8). An unskilful helmsman will make a ship *yaw*.[4]

The Rudder is hung on the stern posts and serves to direct the course of a ship. "This is the bridle which governs the ship."[5] In the face of the enemy:

> Th'Antoniad, the Egyptian admiral,
> With all their sixty, fly and turn the rudder: *Ant. and Cleo*, 3.10.2

Antony, excusing his own flight would have Cleopatra know:

> My heart was to thy rudder tied by the strings. 3.11.57

The Keel is the first timber of a ship to be laid down, and is the groundwork, basis or backbone which unites the whole structure. It was often used as another name for ship. The pirates in *Antony and Cleopatra* have "keels of every kind" (1.4.50); "half the flood Hath their keel cut," describes the progress of Pericles's ship (3 *Chor*. 46).[6]

The Poop was the aftermost and highest deck in an Elizabethan

---

[1] She keeps this figure in a later defiant speech. [2] Mainwaring, Vol. II, p. 164.
[3] Mainwaring, II, 96. [4] See p. 123. [5] Mainwaring, II, 214. [6] Also *Oth*. 2.1.70.

and Jacobean ship. In Cleopatra's barge, "the poop was beaten gold". The most interesting reference to it comes from Falstaff.[1]

The Stem is the foremost main timber of a ship and the Stern the aftermost part outboard. The seamen "skip from stem to stern"—from one end of the ship to the other—in *Pericles*. Such is the power of command of Coriolanus that:

> as weeds before
> A vessel under sail, so men obeyed
> And fell below his stem: 2.2.105

To stem the waves is to make headway against them.[2] Shakespeare coins the word *re-stem* to describe the stratagem of the enemy fleet in *Othello* when it suddenly puts about and heads in a reverse direction. To "give stem to" is to ram or to run against "bows on". A line in 2 *Henry VI*, "turn our stem upon a dreadful rock" (3.2.90), would mean this, but the Folio reading is "stern", making the impact stern first.

The Bishop of Winchester lets it be known that he "will not be Jack out of office" for long, but "sit at chiefest stern of public weal" (1 *Hen. VI* 1.1.177), the steering place being in the stern of a ship.

Sternage is used as a collective term for the sterns of ships in the same way as "anchorage" is for a set of anchors.

> "Grapple your minds to sternage of this navy,"   *Hen. V* 3 Chor. 18

The Timbers of a ship are the ground timbers and the ribs which are scarfed to them. They form the frame besides giving strength to the whole structure.[3] Fears for Othello's safety are met with the assurance:

> "His bark is stoutly timbered."   2.1.48

The Waist is the middle part of a vessel between the upper works forward and the upper works aft (*Temp.* 1.2.197).

RIGGING

The rigging consists of "all the ropes whatsoever, that belong either to a ship's masts, yards or any other part about her".[4]

Prospero is cast adrift in a craft "not rigged", and the Boatswain is amazed to find the King's ship "bravely rigged" when it was believed lost.[5] To rig also had the general meaning of

---

[1] See p. 68.   [2] See pp. 99–114.   [3] See Boat, p. 102.
[4] Boteler, p. 122.   [5] *Tempest*, 1.2.145; 5.1.224.

fit-out. A sense of injury makes Pompey "rig" his navy. Enobarbus announces, "Our great navy's rigged",[1] and Timon of Athens, in his tirade against gold, declaims " 'Tis thou that rigg'st the bark" (5.1.53).

The main ropes of the rigging are the shrouds, stays and tackles.

Shrouds are large ropes which run from the mast head to the sides of the ship. They relieve the masts of lateral strain and enable them to carry sail. This particular use is taken note of in *King John*:

> And all the shrouds wherewith my life should sail
> Are turned to one thread, one little hair:
> My heart hath one poor string to stay it by. 5.7.52

When the wind is high and the shrouds are taut, they make a sound like that of many-stringed instruments, remarkable in range and compass:

> such a noise arose
> As the shrouds make at sea in a stiff tempest,
> As loud, and to as many tunes; *Hen. VIII* 4.1.72

Tackles are ropes of a thinner kind and have various uses. They are made fast to yards and masts to keep them from straining, or are reeved in blocks for heaving. Boat's tackles are for hoisting ship's boats, and gunner's tackles for hauling ordnance. Rope ladders, "cords made like a tackled stair" (*R. and J.* 2.4.182), are of the same rope as tackles. Cleopatra's barge has "silken tackle". Tackle and tackling could mean the ropes of the rigging in general:

> "Upon the hempen tackle ship-boys climbing" *Hen. V* 3 Chor. 8

Lost friends are thought of as "the tackles" of a ship, and those who replace them as "shrouds and tacklings" (3 *Hen. VI* 5.4.15, 18). Elizabeth in *Richard III* is "Like a poor bark, of sails and tackling reft" (4.4.234). King John, nearing his end, "a model of confounded royalty", breathes out in gasps:

> "The tackle of my heart is cracked and burnt" 5.7.51

Coriolanus, even in the threadbare disguise of an exile, is impressive:

> "though thy tackle's torn,
> Thou showest a noble vessel." 4.5.63

[1] *Ant. and Cleo.* 2.6.20; 3.5.19.

This turning to the sea and ships for illustrations, even when there is nothing in the theme itself that is connected with them, is striking, for the wording and working out of likenesses rest on professional knowledge.

ROPE

"Generally all the cordage belonging to a ship is called by the name of rope."[1]

The seaman speaks of "handing" ropes and "handing" sails.

"We will not hand a rope more"   (*Temp.* 1.1.23)

"That which others commonly call pulling a rope the seafaring men call ever hauling."[2] Pericles is thus rightly described as "haling ropes",[3] hale being a variant of haul.

MASTS

The principal masts in a sailing ship are the mainmast, the foremast and the mizzen. The mainmast is the largest and it stands almost amidships. In the storm in the *Winter's Tale*, the ship seems to be "boring the moon with her mainmast". The head of the mainmast is surrounded with a platform known as the maintop. In Imogen's lament, treachery has

From this most bravest vessel of the world
Struck the maintop!   *Cymb.* 4.2.319

Masts in ships of the later sixteenth century rose in three parts or sections, mast, topmast,[4] topgallant mast, which were joined together. Thus, above the mainmast came the main-topmast, above that rose the main topgallant mast, and so with the foremast and mizzen. Romeo, in giving directions, explains that a rope ladder:

. . . to the high topgallant of my joy
Must be my convoy.   2.4.183

The topgallant was the highest mast of all until, in the later seventeenth century, the topgallant-royal was raised at its head.

An additional mast was the Boltsprit or Bowsprit, a large

[1] Mainwaring, Vol. II, p. 212.   [2] Mainwaring, Vol. II, p. 161.
[3] See p. 42.   [4] See p. 38.

boom projecting at an angle over the stem. Ariel flamed "distinctly on the topmast, yards and bowsprit".

When masts were lost in a storm or "carried by the board" in a fight, a yard could be rigged instead and this was known as a jury-mast. Shakespeare, without using the name, describes it as:

> a small spare mast,
> Such as seafaring men provide for storms. *C. of E.* 1.1.78

For giving "way and steerage" to a ship, it was considered "a poor shift in case of necessity",[1] but, in the *Comedy of Errors*, it proved a means of saving life.[2]

The height of the masts of sailing ships, "the high and giddy mast", was, and has remained, one of the remarkable things about them, and masts were taken as a measure when attempting to give some idea of drops and heights:

> Ten masts at each make not the altitude
> Which thou has perpendicularly fell. *K. Lear* 4.6.54

Even today, the masts of the *Victory* tower above those of all other ships in Portsmouth harbour.

The Yards take their names from the masts to which they belong and are "those long pieces which are fashioned somewhat small towards the ends, and they hang cross-wise upon the masts".[3]

OARS

The *Oar* is a long wooden lever used to row or propel a boat, and its parts are known as blade, loom and handle.

In Cleopatra's barge:

> the oars were silver,
> Which to the tune of flutes kept stroke, and made
> The water which they beat to follow faster,
> As amorous of their strokes. 2.2.194

Here, music sets the rhythm of the stroke, in contrast to what happens in Marvell's verses on the emigrants in Bermuda, where it is the rhythm of the oars that sets the time of the song which echoes "beyond the Mexique bay":

> Thus sung they in the English boat
> A holy and a cheerful note:
> And all the way, to guide their chime,
> With falling oars they kept the time.

[1] Boteler, p. 117.   [2] See p. 44.   [3] Boteler, p. 113. See Sail, p. 114.

The arms of a swimmer are likened to oars,[1] so also are the fins of a fish:

> see the fish
> Cut with her golden oars the silver stream. *Much Ado* 3.1.27

RIBS

The Ribs are the curved frame timbers of a ship extending from the keel to the top of the hull. They form the skeleton to which the planking of the sides is secured.

> What ribs of oak, when mountains melt on them,
> Can hold the mortise? *Oth.* 2.1.8

exclaims a watcher ashore as he looks out on mountainous seas breaking over a labouring ship. "Mortise" is a shipwright's term, being the name for the holes cut in one piece of timber to let in another and so form a joint. The ribs of a ship are joined in this way.

In the *Merchant of Venice*, a bark returns from a voyage with "over-weathered ribs" (2.6.18), but of greater interest are the lines:

> And see my wealthy Andrew docked in sand,
> Vailing her high top lower then her ribs,
> To kiss her burial. 1.1.28

Monson and eight of his company were prisoners, strongly guarded, in the castle of Lisbon and he tells how, on St. Andrew's day, 1591:

> "being upon the walls at our usual hour, we beheld a great galleon of the King's turning up the river in her fighting sails, being sumptuously decked with ancients, streamers and pendants, with all other ornaments to shew her bravery. She let fly all her ordnance in a triumphant manner for the taking of Sir Richard Greynvile in the Revenge at the island of Flores, she being one of that fleet and the first voyage she ever made.
>
> "I confess it was one of the greatest and sorrowfullest sights that ever my eyes beheld to see the cause the Spaniards had to boast, and no remedy in me to revenge it but in my tongue, but hoped for future comfort, and took such Englishmen as were in my company to witness what I should say to them: I offered to give them one for ten, if I did live to be at the

---

[1] See Swimming, p. 134.

taking and possessing of that triumphant galleon, that carried the name of that day, viz. St. Andrew."[1]

Five years later, Monson had his wish. In the raid on Cadiz by Essex and Raleigh (1596), he was captain of the *Repulse* and took part in the capture of the *St. Andrew* and brought her to Chatham. But in passing through the King's Channel, he "endured more foul weather and trouble than in the whole voyage besides, by reason of the unwieldiness of the St. Andrew when she came to work in the narrow channel among the sands".[2] The proud ship might well have become "docked in sand, . . . vailing her high top lower than her ribs, To kiss her burial". When she was added to the Fleet and took part in the Islands Voyage of 1597, Essex had fears that what had occurred at Chatham would happen again, and, in a despatch to the Queen, asking permission "to anchor under the Isle of Wight and there to attend for direction", urged as his main reason, "I do humbly beseech her Majesty to think how dangerous it will be for her great ships to go about the Sands this ill-time of the year, especially for the St. Andrew!"[3]

The vessel was of more than usual interest and was one of the sights down the river, and later at Portsmouth, as the *St. Matthew*, another prize, had been at La Rochelle.[4] This is reflected in the allusion. The wording, "docked", "vailing", "high top", "ribs" is technical. In oozy or sandy ground, "when a ship hath made herself by her ponderousness a hollow place to lie in, she is said in sea language to have docked herself".[5] Vailing is part of naval ceremony.[6]

SAILS

Sails are "large pieces of doubled canvas which, when they are spread abroad, do catch the wind and so give way, that is, give motion to the ships".[7]

Sails take their names from the masts, yards and stays on which they are spread; the mainsail from the mainmast, the main-topsail from the main-topmast, the main-topgallant sail from the main-topgallant mast, and so in turn with the foremast and the

---

[1] Monson, Vol. V, p. 172.   [2] Monson, Vol. I, p. 357.   [3] Calendar of the Manuscripts . . . Preserved at Hatfield House, Historical Manuscripts Commission, Vol. VII (1899), p. 440.
[4] Monson, Vol. II, p. 57.   [5] Boteler, p. 145.   [6] See p. 22.   [7] Boteler, p. 113.

mizzen. The lower sails are known as courses. The main-course is the mainsail.[1] Sails are made fast to the yards which are heaved up and down on the masts.

The management of the sails requires great skill and is one of the most exacting tests of seamanship. Shakespeare understands the principles of sail and uses many technical sailing terms. To *hoise* or *hoist* is the term for drawing up the sails on the masts and stays. Richmond "Hoised sail and made his course again for Brittany" (*R. III* 4.4.529). "Will you hoist sail, sir?", asks Maria, and is given a very professional answer.[2] Cleopatra "Hoists sails and flies" (3.10.15).[3]

A ship, loosed from her moorings and under control of her sails and rudder, is said to be "under sail". This is always used strictly: "He came too late, the ship was under sail"(*M. of V.* 2.8.6 and 2.6.68), "the false Troyan under sail was seen" (*M.N.D.* 1.1.174), "The ship is under sail, and here she comes amain" (*L.L.L.* 5.2.549).

Prospero's words in the Epilogue to *The Tempest*:

> Gentle breath of yours my sails
> Must fill, or else my project fails   5 *Ep.* 11–12

are technical as well as poetical. To "fill" a sail, the wind must enter it from behind, its force being exerted in such a way that the ship moves ahead:[4]

> As doth a sail, fill'd with a fretting gust
> Command an argosy to stem the waves.   3 *Hen. VI* 2.6.35

The sail is then said to be "full":

> Was it the proud full sail of his great verse,
> Bound for the prize of all too precious you.   *Sonnet 86*

"Full sail" is not to be confused with "under full canvas" which is the sea phrase for having all sails abroad. "Blown" is also used in the sense of "full":

> Toward Ephesus
> Turn our blown sails: *Per.* 5.1.252

"Calmed," a variant of becalmed, describes a ship when there is no wind to fill her sails or when the wind is kept from her by another ship or by the land:

> Like to a ship that, having scap'd a tempest,
> Is straightway calmed, and boarded with a pirate.   2 *Hen. VI* 4.9.33

[1] See p. 38.   [2] See p. 106.   [3] Also *C. of E.* 5.1.21; *Sonnet 117.*
[4] "Swell" is used for "fill" in *Oth.* 2.1.78.

Iago, after Cassio's promotion, likens his position to that of a ship under the lee of another "belee'd and calmed". *Belee'd*, an unusual form, is a coinage and is made up in a way that follows a fashion of the day (*Oth.* 1.1.30).

"Tacking" or going about or fetching about, one of the most important manoeuvres in sailing, is briefly described in two lines which, like King John's later talk of shrouds and tackle, are in "the words of the art":

> And like a *shifted* wind unto a *sail*
> It makes the *course* of thoughts to *fetch about*.   *K. John* 4.2.23

Tacking is to bring a ship's head to lie the other way: "If her head lay first west-north-west now it must lie east-north-east, the wind being at north."[1]

In rough weather, the Bowline or Bollin, a *rope* fastened to the leech or middle part of a sail to make it stand sharp or close by a wind, is eased in preparation for taking in sail. Hence the order, "Sack the bolins there!" as the storm grows worse in *Pericles* (3.1.43).

To loof[2] is to make a ship keep close to the wind and is used of Cleopatra's vessel quitting the fight: "She once being looft" (3.10.18).

"Clap on more sails; pursue,"[3] is an order to set more sail and so increase speed. Antony "claps on his seawing" and follows in the wake of Cleopatra. It has the same meaning as "crack on" in the Royal Navy today. It could also mean to attach one tackle to another or to a rope and it still does.

The different parts of a sail, such as the leech and clew, are not referred to, but "shoulder" in:

> "The wind sits in the shoulder of your sail"   *Ham.* 1.3.56

seems to be another name for the "bunt" which is "the very pouch, or bag of a sail; . . . the better to catch and hold the wind".[4]

To strike is to lower a sail. In rough weather, sails may be "struck" or taken in:

> we hear this fearful tempest sing,
> Yet seek no shelter to avoid the storm;
> We see the wind sit sore upon our sails,
> And yet we strike not, but securely perish.   *R. II* 2.1.263

---

[1] Mainwaring, Vol. II, p. 241.
[2] See p. 69.
[3] See p. 10. The reading in the First Folio is correct.
[4] Boteler, p. 120.

Striking and vailing are also part of naval ceremony.[1]

Sail, like keel, may have the sense of ship:

> "I have sixty sails, Caesar none better"; "Forgive my fearful sails!"; "Swallows have built In Cleopatra's sails their nests."[2]

It is not restricted to ships descried at a distance: "they cry, A sail!"[3]

[1] See p. 22.   [2] *Ant. and Cleo.* 3.7.50, 3.11.55, 4.12.4.   [3] *Oth.* 2.1.54; also 2.1.4, 51, 93.

GUNNERY

Heavy guns were introduced in royal ships by Henry VIII. This led to great changes in naval warfare in which England came to take the lead.

The King of Spain's instructions to Medina Sidonia made clear what the Armada would have to be prepared to face: "You are especially to take notice that the enemy's object will be to engage at a distance, on account of the advantage which they have from their artillery and the offensive fireworks with which they will be provided; and on the other hand, the object on our side should be to close and grapple and engage hand to hand."[1]

But this kind of warfare which depended on boarding and assault was, in the eyes of the English admirals, out of date, and Raleigh, writing much later on the advantage of engaging the enemy at a distance with well-directed fire, maintained: "In like sort had the lord Charles Howard, admiral of England, been lost in the year 1588 ... had he entangled himself with those great and powerful vessels."[2]

English guns came to be in such demand all over Europe during the greater part of the reign of Elizabeth and in the early seventeenth century that efforts were made by Orders in Council, and in other ways, to prevent the export of ordnance. "But such has been the oversight of some magistrates in times past that they have connived at the transportation of our English ordnance, which exceeds all other in Europe for goodness. And now no country, from the hithermost parts to the uttermost bounds of the world, but is able to give testimony of it in their forts and castles, which are stuffed and fortified with them, to the unspeakable hazard and danger to ourselves."[3]

Instruction of a high standard was essential, but foreign manuals had to be used until 1578 when William Bourne published *The Arte of Shooting in great Ordnaunce*: "I am the first Englishman that put forth any booke as touching the art of gunnery.'

[1] *The Defeat of the Spanish Armada*, Vol. I, l.   [2] *The Works of Sir Walter Ralegh, Kt.* 1829), 8 vols., Vol. 6, pp. 81–82. (*The History of the World*, Bk. V, Chap. I, Sec. vi.)
[3] Monson, Vol. IV, pp. 44–45.

Within the next ten years, English gunnery, particularly at sea, came to be unrivalled. It is not surprising to find Shakespeare showing considerable interest in ordnance and guns when they had changed the whole character of naval warfare and brought safety and triumph to England. "A gunner must know the names of his pieces."[1] Shakespeare distinguishes between various types of ordnance and gun, understands how they work and are managed, and is familiar with gunnery terms and words of command.

A "piece" of ordnance, as it was called, was "mounted" or put on its "carriage".

"A piece of ordnance 'gainst it I have placed," says the Master-Gunner of Orleans, when instructing his boy to keep watch (1 *Hen. VI* 1.4.15).

> Behold the ordnance on their carriages,
> With fatal mouths gaping on girded Harfleur

is part of the scene of siege in *Henry V* (3 Chor. 26). In *King John*,[2] cannon are "ready mounted . . . to spit forth Their iron indignation" (2.1.211) and:

> France and England mount
> Their battering cannon charged to the mouths. 2.1.381

The order to the gunners was "Give fire", and this Pistol uses in the *Merry Wives of Windsor* (2.2.126) and in 2 *Hen. IV* (2.4.178). The linstock, a long, forked stave holding a lighted match, was then applied to the powder:

> the nimble gunner
> With linstock now the devilish cannon touches. *Hen. V* 3 Chor. 32

The discharge of the shot followed,

> As violently as hasty powder fired
> Doth hurry from the fatal cannon's womb *R. and J.* 5.1.63

is how Romeo, wearied of life, hopes that his body may be "discharged of breath".

Cannon went off with thunderous noise:

> I am vanquished; these haughty words of hers
> Have battered me like roaring cannon shot 1 *Hen. VI* 3.3.78

describes the effect of Joan of Arc's speech on the Duke of Burgundy.

[1] Monson, Vol. IV, p. 35.   [2] See p. 20, note 1, and p. 25, note 1.

Smoke accompanied the shattering roar:

> As smoke from Aetna, that in air consumes,
> Or that which from discharged cannon fumes.   *Lucr.* 1043

The whole operation colours the ingenious talk of Armado and Moth in *Love's Labour's Lost*:

> Sweet smoke of rhetoric!
> He reputes me a cannon, and the bullet, that's he —— 3.1.60

Cannon are said to shoot point blank when pointing or aiming straight at the mark in the horizontal level position. Fleet orders directed that, "The gunners shall not shoot any great ordnance at other distance than point blank."[1] Cade tells Lord Say, "Now art thou within point blank of our jurisdiction regal" (*2 Hen. VI* 4.7.23). Falstaff's page "will carry a letter twenty mile, as easy as a cannon will shoot point blank twelve score!" (*M. Wives* 3.2.23). It is the King's hope in *Hamlet*, in his words of dismay to the Queen, that slander:

> As level as the cannon to his blank
> Transports his poisoned shot, may miss our name,
> And hit the woundless air.   4.1.41

Desdemona has "stood within the blank" of Othello's displeasure for her "free speech" on Cassio's behalf (3.4.126).

Most effective of all at sea was the broadside which is the discharge of all the ship's guns on one side:

> "Fear we broadsides? No, let the fiend give fire."   2 *Hen. IV* 2.4.178

The recoil or rebound of ordnance and firearms had its dangers, and these were greatly increased when the piece had been overcharged. This is used as a forcible illustration to bring home to Suffolk that his "dread curses" may:

> like an overcharged gun, recoil
> And turn the force of them upon thyself.   2 *Hen. VI* 3.2.330

Other accidents could arise from failure to guard powder from exposure to flame. Friar Lawrence tells Romeo that intemperate emotion is marring his judgement which,

> Like powder in a skilless soldier's flask
> Is set afire by thine own ignorance,
> And thou dismembered with thine own defence.   *R. and J.* 3.3.132

Cannon were distinguished by various names, and not, as later, by the weight of the shot they carried. Shakespeare refers only to cannon, demi cannon, basilisk, and culverin, but there were others: serpentine, saker, minion, falcon and falconet.

[1] *Fighting Instructions 1530–1816*, p. 41.

"Thou hast talked . . . of basilisks, of cannon, culverin," says Lady Percy to Hotspur, as she seeks to learn the cause of his unrest (1 *Hen. IV* 2.3.55). The Basilisk was a large cannon usually of brass. It took its name from the fabled serpent whose eyes were supposed to kill with a look. Though Isabel, Queen of France, has the serpent in mind when she refers to the eyes of Henry V, bent on France, as:

> "The fatal balls of murdering basilisks,"   *Hen. V* 5.2.17

the words carry a double meaning.

The Culverin is mentioned by name alone and only once. It was one of the large types of cannon, long in proportion to its bore, for it was mistakenly held that this added to the force of the shot. The Demi cannon, made on the same principle, was in length about twenty-five times the diameter of the bore. Petruchio, in the *Taming of the Shrew*, is reminded of it by the curiously cut trunk sleeve of his wife's new gown:

> What's this? a sleeve? 't is like a demi cannon.
> What, up and down, carved like an apple tart?   4.3.88

The Mortar piece, a short piece of ordnance with a large bore, was a kind of pot gun.

"He stands there, like a mortarpiece, to blow us," is said of a formidable doorkeeper who looks as if he were ready to blow everyone up—"a 'firedrake' who should be a brazier by his face" (*Hen. VIII* 5.3.42 ff.). Wildfire, a composition of inflammable materials, difficult to extinguish, was often shot out of mortar pieces. Sinon's

> . . . words like wildfire burnt the shining glory
> Of rich-built Ilion.   *Lucrece* 1523

The Murdering-piece or Murder was a small piece of ordnance, of iron or brass, with chambers that discharged old iron, stones, bullets and various missiles which flew in all directions. It could be almost as dangerous to those who fired as to those who were aimed at. Its effect is well described by the King in *Hamlet*:

> This,
> Like to a murdering piece, in many places
> Gives me superfluous death.   4.5.95

The Petar or Petard, a metal container, filled with gunpowder and fired by a fuse, was used to blow in doors or gates or to make a breach in walls. Hamlet, in planning to outwit knavery, muses:

> For 'tis the sport to have the enginer
> Hoist with his own petar;   3.4.206 ff.

or, in more modern words, blown up by his own bomb. And, with the strategy of besieging and undermining in mind, he goes on:

> and 't shall go hard
> But I will delve one yard below their mines,
> And blow them at the moon.

He again turns to the language of gunnery after the pirate incident and tells Horatio:

> I have words to speak in thine ear will make thee dumb;
> yet are they much too light for the bore of the matter   4.6.26

meaning that they will be like small shot in a gun of large calibre.

Gun is used in a wide sense. It may mean any firearm including the sportman's gun and the fowler's gun:

> ... russet-pated choughs, many in sort,
> Rising and cawing at the gun's report,
> Sever themselves and madly sweep the sky   *M.N.D.* 3.2.22

or else ordnance, as when the foppish messenger, who provokes Hotspur, says:

> but for these vile guns,
> He would himself have been a soldier.   1 *Hen. IV* 1.3.62

The Pistol is a small firearm, held in one hand, and fired in that way. Douglas "rides at high speed, and with his pistol kills a sparrow flying" (1 *Hen. IV* 2.4.340). In the *Merry Wives of Windsor*, "three of Master Ford's brothers watch the door with pistols", adding to Falstaff's alarm and to the comedy (4.2.46).

The weapon gives rise to some play on Pistol's name. "It sorts well with your fierceness," Henry V tells him (*Hen. V* 4.1.63). "Pistol, I will double charge thee with dignities" is Falstaff's boast on hearing that Henry V is king (2 *Hen. IV* 5.3.130).

The setting of *Pericles* with its voyaging and naval ceremony is Elizabethan, and Thaliard is kept in line with this when, scorning poison as a means of carrying out his overlord's order, he assures him:

> My lord, if I can get him within my pistol's
> length, I'll make him sure enough.   1.1.167

The Caliver, a small handgun or harquebus, went off with a sharp bang. Falstaff's recruits "fear the report of a caliver worse than a struck fowl or a hurt wild-duck" (1 *Hen. IV* 4.2.18). Bardolph and he undertake to instruct one of them in the handling of this weapon:

Falstaff.   Put me a caliver into Wart's hand, Bardolph.
Bardolph. Hold, Wart, traverse! thus, thus, thus.
Falstaff.   Come, manage me your caliver. So: very well: go to: very good:
           exceeding good. . . . Hold, there's a tester for thee."

                                              2 Hen. IV 3.2.269

It would be interesting to have the comments of a gunner of
the day on their methods of instruction.

The Musket, though mentioned only once in Shakespeare, was
found serviceable at sea. "As for such fiery weapons as are
managed by single men, and to be used above the decks, I
know none fitter than the ordinary musket."[1] But it is with land
warfare in mind that Helena thinks of Bertram as driven "to be
the mark of smoky muskets" (*All's Well* 3.2.108).

Shakespeare's readiness in bringing in gunnery, and in making
apt use of it even in figures of speech, points to much wider
professional knowledge than the examples themselves show.

Hamlet

Hamlet shows aptness in the terms of other arts and professions
besides gunnery, and this is one of Shakespeare's ways of por-
traying a character that, far from being self-absorbed or stolid, is
responsive and quickly affected by different people and by what
is going on around him. He speaks to the players in the idiom of
the stage, and he is nautical in his report on the pirates and in the
account of his voyage which he introduces with a reference to one
of the customary punishments aboard a warship:

                    methought I lay
          Worse than the mutines in the bilboes,   5.2.5 ff.

"The punishment at the bilboes is when a delinquent is put
in irons, or in a kind of stocks made for that purpose, the
which are more or less heavy and pinching, as the quality of
the offence is found to be, upon good proof."[2]

The rest of the story follows:

                      up from my cabin
          My sea-gown scarfed about me, in the dark
          Groped I.

He returns to sea terms at a later point to outdo Osric whose
affected style, suggesting voyaging with its play on "card",

---

[1] Boteler, p. 261.   [2] Boteler, p. 17.

"calendar" and "continent", is annoying him. Hamlet does not make his technical words easy for his hearer.

> "I know to divide him inventorially would dizzy the arithmetic of memory, and yet but yaw neither in respect of his quick sail."
>
> 5.2.117.

What, it may be asked, does he mean? Osric's recitation of the merits of Laertes makes Hamlet think of the kind of detail found in inventories of ships which, in their minuteness, read like surveyors' reports. The "Inventarie of the Shyp Ayde"[1] is a good example. Furthermore, mathematics came to be of great importance in navigation from about 1580: "this sweete skill of sayling may well be called Navigation arithmeticall, because it wholy consisteth of Calculations."[2] These calculations proved rather formidable, but grew less so as new ways of making them were found, and when Napier's logarithms appeared in 1614, "dizzying" of the memory, as it is called here, belonged to the past, for it was rightly claimed that this invention "doth cleane take away all the difficultie that heretofore hath beene".[3] To complete this picture of toiling effort outstripped or defeated, yawing is brought in:

> "When a ship is not steered steady, but she goes in and out with her head, they say she yaws. This doth much hinder a ship's way."[4]

What Horatio makes of their exchanges comes out in his comment:

> "Is't not possible to understand in another tongue?"   5.2.128

---

[1] *The Three Voyages of Martin Frobisher*, edited by Richard Collinson (1867), Hakluyt Society Series I, Vol. 38, p. 218.   [2] *The Seamans Secrets*, by John Davis (1595), n.p. K3.   [3] *Mirifici Logarithmorum Canonis descriptio*, by John Napier, Baron Merchiston, Edinburgh (1614).   [4] Mainwaring, Vol. II, p. 259.

WAVES

Ocean waves result from the action of the wind on the surface of the water. When first formed, they are short and steep, but if the wind continues to blow in the same direction for a considerable time, their length and height increase.

Though scientific description is not part of Shakespeare's purpose, he can come near to it when using some of the sea terms that were then applied to waves. "Bold" meaning steep is one. It has nothing to do with fearlessness or audacity, but almost invites play on words and does lead to it in "make his bold waves tremble" (*Temp*. 1.2.205). "Tumbling",[1] meaning rolling, and "yesty" for frothy like yeast are others.

Words like "overmatching", "contentious", "inconstant" and "wild" describe the turbulent action of waves but are not nautical. Most frequent are words that have nothing to do with what waves are in themselves but convey feelings about them— blind, ruthless, ruffian, chidden—that might arise in an onlooker.

The wind has its greatest effect on the crest of waves, tending to drive them faster than the main body and thus causing them to break. In a violent wind, "spindrift", a sort of driving spray, is swept from their tops and is carried along the surface of the water, flying like a vapour or rising in clouds:

> the winds
> Who take the ruffian billows by the top,
> Curling their monstrous heads and hanging them
> With deaf'ning clamour in the slippery clouds.   2 *Hen. VI* 3.1.21

Waves have a well-defined motion. As rapidly as those in front die out, new waves rise behind them and this gives uniformity to the general appearance of a group.

> Like as the waves make towards the pebbled shore,
> So do our minutes hasten to their end;
> Each changing place with that which goes before,
> In sequent toil all forwards do contend.   *Sonnet 60*

Deep-sea waves are changed in character as they reach shoal water where there may not be enough depth for a complete

---

[1] *R. III* 1.4.20.

wave to be formed. The bottom of the wave is retarded by the friction of the sea-bed and the top is thrown forward so that it breaks into surf or foam, as in the lines on the sea-coast of Dardan:

> their ranks began
> To break upon the galled shore, and than
> Retire again, till meeting greater ranks
> They join, and shoot their foam at Simois' banks.   *Lucrece* 1439

"When it overblows . . . exceedingly",[1]

> the yesty waves
> Confound and swallow navigation up.   *Macb.* 4.1.53

A wave or billow, in Shakespeare's day, was often named a surge. "We call a wave a surge."[2] Characters speak of "the surges" and of "the wind-shaked surge".[3] Besides this general sense, it had a particular meaning—"those are especially termed surges which beat and break upon the shores",[4] and this is also found in the plays:

> "surge that on the unnumbered idle pebbles chafes."
>
> *K. Lear* 4.6.20[5]

Surge is now a term for heavy tidal surges or seiches which are associated with volcanoes, earthquakes and hurricanes. They can be caused artificially by nuclear explosions under water designed to create giant waves that could flood out the country of an enemy.

[1] Mainwaring, Vol. II, p. 243.   [2] Mainwaring, p. 240.
[3] *T.N.* 5.1.236; *Oth.* 2.1.13; also *Per.* 3.1.1; *Tit. And.* 3.1.96; *T. of A.* 4.2.21; *Cymb.* 3.1.28; *Temp.* 2.1.114.   [4] Boteler, p. 238.   [5] Also *T. of A.* 4.3.444.

WATERSPOUTS

Waterspouts were often given the name "hurricano" by seamen, because they result from the same kind of conditions in the atmosphere as whirlwinds and tornadoes. Shakespeare, in using both names, takes note of the force of these spouts and of how they appear to descend from clouds overhanging the surface of the sea. He also accepts views held at the time about the part played by the heat of the sun in their formation.

> Not the dreadful spout,[1]
> Which shipmen do the hurricane call,
> Constringed in mass by the almighty sun,
> Shall dizzy with more clamour Neptune's ear
> In his descent than shall my prompted sword
> Falling on Diomed.   *Troil. and Cres.* 5.2.171

The Captain in Boteler's *Dialogues* describes how they work, and speaks of the havoc they can cause in a way that bears out what Shakespeare says:

> "As for Spouts, they are those sudden and mighty falls of water, which pillar-wise fall from a cloud at the breaking of it; and these are found in most hot countries and especially in the West Indies; and are sometimes in such abundance that if they unluckily light in a ship . . . it would endanger her foundering right down in the sea." [2]

[1] See *K. Lear* 3.2.2.
[2] Boteler, p. 243, See also Hakluyt, Vol. VI, (1904), p. 171.

PROMONTORIES

Steep and windy headlands, broad sea-capes, cliffs gleaming in the sunlight or half-swathed in mist stand out in heroic tales of ocean-going in early English epic, or form a background to that lorn sense of the hardness of man's lot and of the fleetingness of life that pervades its elegy and lament. The vistas that promontories open lead to visions of the boundless that seem to beckon, and stir feelings of wistfulness, longing and yearning or of aspiration or resolve:

> Like one that stands upon a promontory,
> And spies a far-off shore where he would tread,
> Wishing his foot were equal with his eye:
> And chides the sea that sunders him from thence,
> Saying, he'll lade it dry to have his way.   3 *Hen. VI* 3.2.135

Horror and a haunting awareness of being on the verge of the dread unknown cling to the sea-cliff in *Hamlet*. All is ominous, the night hour, the remoteness of the place, the precipitous drop and the wrathful sound of the ocean:

> What if it tempt you toward the flood, my lord,
> Or to the dreadful summit of the cliff
> That beetles o'er his base into the sea,
> The very place puts toys of desperation
> Without more motive, into every brain
> That looks so many fathoms to the sea
> And hears it roar beneath.   1.4.69

Dover cliff is unmatched as a living, moving picture of an abiding England—the chalky bourn, the murmuring surge, the choughs that wing the midway air, the shrill gorged lark, the fishermen that walk upon the beach, the tall anchoring bark.

Edgar unfolds it all to his blind father who, feeling that there is no longer anything to live for, has sought the cliff only as a way of bringing his wretchedness to an end:

> There is a cliff, whose high and bending head
> Looks fearfully in the confined deep:
> Bring me but to the very brim of it,
> And I'll repair the misery thou dost bear
> With something rich about me: from that place
> I shall no leading need.   4.1.73

Edgar, unrecognised, sets himself to play upon natural fears and the recoil that goes with them:

> How fearful
> And dizzy 'tis to cast one's eyes so low!
> I'll look no more,
> Lest my brain turn, and the deficient sight
> Topple down headlong.　4.6.11 ff.

But he seeks to win back attachment to life at the same time, and this scene of men at their tasks, the sea and ships, birds on the wing and much else that stirs love of country is meant to work in that way:

> The crows, and choughs, that wing the midway air
> Show scarce so gross as beetles: halfway down
> Hangs one that gathers samphire, dreadful trade!
> Methinks he seems no bigger than his head.
> The fishermen, that walk upon the beach,
> Appear like mice; and yond tall anchoring bark,
> Diminished to her cock, her cock, a buoy
> Almost too small for sight. The murmuring surge,
> That on the unnumbered idle pebbles chafes,
> Cannot be heard so high.　4.6.13 ff.

To make sure that his father will live on, Edgar leads him to believe that he has leapt over and been miraculously preserved: "Why I do trifle thus with his despair Is done to cure it."

> Hadst thou been aught but gossamer, feathers, air,
> So many fathom down precipitating,
> Thou'dst shivered like an egg: but thou dost breathe,
> Hast heavy substance, bleed'st not, speak'st, art sound.
> Ten masts at each make not the altitude
> Which thou hast perpendicularly fell:
> Thy life's a miracle. Speak yet again.　4.6.49

In this tense drama which springs from what lies at the roots of human nature, the cliff becomes almost like a character, working, as it does, on feelings and thoughts and having an influence of its own on what is done.

FISHERMEN

Fishermen recover Pericles's armour from the sea in their nets, and enable him to go to Court and take part in a tournament in which he wins his wife. This could be reported in a few lines, but what might have been little more than a brief connecting link, is made into an original scene by Shakespeare.[1] The fishermen are well drawn. Industrious and practical, their good nature, no less than their good sense, strikes Pericles.

> "How well this honest mirth becomes their labour."

They are also humane and are distressed by the shipwreck:

Third. I am thinking of the poor men that were cast away before us even now.

First. Alas, poor souls, it grieved my heart to hear what pitiful cries they made to us to help them, when, well-a-day, we could scarce help ourselves.

They show themselves shrewd but just critics of the state of the nation, speaking of the good things as well as the ills of their times:

> How from the finny subject of the sea
> These fishers tell the infirmities of men:

As Jacobeans, they know that their wellbeing springs from the "peaceable reign and good government" of the king, but oppressors, and wealth that comes unearned and without effort, are not unknown, and they would be glad to see the monarch "purge the land of these drones, that rob the bee of her honey". The law, too, can be slow in its working and justice may be long delayed: "here's a fish hangs in the net, like a poor man's right in the law; 't will hardly come out."

But there is also prosperity and plenty as the generous hospitality they offer shows:

> "come, thou shalt go home, and we'll have flesh for holidays, fish for fasting days, and moreo'er puddings and flapjacks; and thou shalt be welcome."

Many proclamations were issued in the reigns of Elizabeth, James I and Charles I, in support of the statute of Edward VI,

---

[1] *Pericles* Act II, sc. 1, 12 ff.

enacting that Fridays and Saturdays, Ember Days and Lent were to be kept as fish days, and these are reflected here. Small books and pamphlets also appeared at intervals for over half a century suggesting measures that might be taken to increase the national wealth by encouraging fishing. "The Petty Navy Royal", by John Dee in 1576,[1] gave some attention to this, but more important was "A Politic Plat", by Robert Hitchcock in 1580.[2]

Hitchcock invited "the Burgesses of almost all the stately Port Towns of England and Wales" to dine with him at Westminster and put before them a scheme for borrowing eighty thousand pounds by a levy to be repaid within three years.[3] The money was to provide fishing vessels for some two hundred and twenty-five dwindling towns in England and Wales to lessen or end unemployment and to ensure that those who were out of work through no fault of their own would be enabled to prove their usefulness, while at the same time, vagabonds would be given a chance to "labour willingly" and show themselves "good subjects, and profitable members of this common weal".[4] The Speaker of the Commons thought highly of the plan and said, "A Parliament hath been called for a less cause". Hitchcock himself was almost carried away as he contemplated the benefits that would follow:

> "such a number of carpenters and shipwrights set on work; such a number of coopers employed; such numbers of people making lines, ropes, and cables; dressers of hemp, spinners of thread, and makers of nets; so many salt houses set up to make salt, and 'salt upon salt'. And what a number of mariners are made of poor men, and what a number of poor men are set on work in those shires all along upon the sea coast in England and Wales in splitting of fish, washing of fish, packing of fish, salting of fish, carrying and recarrying of fish, and serving all the counties in England with fish. And to serve all those occupations aforesaid, there must depend an infinite number of servants, boys, and day labourers, for the use of things needful."[5]

A further aim was to increase, by many thousands, the reserves of mariners for the safeguard of the country.

Those for whom no work could be found, and who were begging

leave to toil, were carefully distinguished from rogues, vagrants
and complacent sturdy beggars.

> "For the heart, mind, and value of a man is such, and his
> spirit is so great, that he will travel all the kingdoms of Princes
> to seek entertainment; rather than he will show his face to beg
> or crave relief of thousands of people, that be unworthy to
> unbuckle his shoes: and in his great want, will take with force
> and courage from them that hath, to serve his necessity;
> thinking it more happy to die speedily, than to live defamed and
> miserably. Of which sort of people, at the breaking up of wars,
> there are a great number of worthy and valiant soldiers, that
> have served in the wars with invincible minds:"[1]

Similar concern over this state of things, and uneasiness about
those who suffered from it underlie Pericles's words to the
fishermen: "He asks of you, that never used to beg," and the
bitterness of being dependent comes out when he is driven to
say:

> What I have been I have forgot to know
> But what I am, want teaches me to think on.

But the master fisherman does not allow him to feel obliged:

> "No, friend cannot you beg? here's them in our country . . . gets
> more with begging than we can do with working"

and he makes all well by the way in which he adds,

> "I have a gown here, come, put it on; keep thee warm. Now, afore
> me, a handsome fellow!"

The incident ends in a lighter strain, with some play on the
meaning of "beg" and "crave", as the second fisherman rallies
Pericles on his good fortune:

Fisherman. Hark you, my friend; you said you could not beg.
Pericles. I did but crave.
Fisherman. But crave? then I'll turn craver too, and so I shall 'scape whipping.

Whipping was a regular punishment for beggars.

These early works were followed by "England's Way to Win
Wealth and to employ Ships and Mariners", by Tobias Gentleman, in 1614[2] and *Britain's Buss,* by E.S. in 1615.[3]

> "No fisher but the ungrown fry forbears." *Ven. and Adon.* 525

---

[1] *An English Garner,* by Edward Arber, Vol. II, pp. 160–61.
[2] *An English Garner,* Vol. IV, pp. 323–49.   [3] *An English Garner,* Vol. III, pp. 621–56.

This unwritten law, which Shakespeare sums up in a line, was not always observed. "There are too too many of those pernicious Trinkermen, who with trinker-boats destroy the river of Thames, by killing the fry and small fish there, even all that comes to net, before it be either meat or marketable. Which Trinkermen (if they will not offer themselves) may, by order and authority of our State, be compelled to give over that evil, and to follow this good trade."[1] The problem remains an international one.

[1] *An English Garner*, Vol. III, p. 650.

SWIMMING

The only manuals of swimming in Shakespeare's age were Everard Digby's *De Arte Natandi*, 1587, in Latin and an adaptation in English by Christofer Middleton entitled, *A Short introduction for to learne to Swimme, Gathered out of Master Digbies Booke of the Art of Swimming*, 1595.[1]

Swimming, like watermanship, horsemanship or archery, was treated as one of those exercises "whereby should growe both recreation and profite".[2] Swimming was particularly favoured, "it being so profitable a thing as it is towards the preserving of mans lyfe when as he is at any time distressed in the greedie iawes of the swelling Sea".[3]

The opening part of Middleton's book, very much condensed from Digby, deals with the art of swimming in general and the rest of the work consists of interesting diagrams with brief directions for various exercises and feats such as, to swim on the back, to swim with hands and feet upward, to swim like a dolphin, to beat the water, to sit in the water, to seek anything that is lost in the water, to swim under the water.

The descriptions of swimming found in Shakespeare could come only from one who understood the art. He is aware of the fatal mistakes that the inexperienced or the exhausted are most likely to make, knowing how:

> an unpractised swimmer plunging still,
> With too much labour drowns for want of skill   *Lucrece* 1098

and realising the hopeless plight of:

> two spent swimmers, that so cling together
> And choke their art.   *Macbeth* 1.2.8

Using the swimming terms of the time, he gives a vivid and technically accurate account of how Ferdinand, after leaping overboard and plunging into the foaming sea, swims strongly for shore:

> I saw him *beat* the surges under him,
> And ride upon their backs, he *trod* the water,
> Whose enmity he flung aside, and *breasted*

---

[1] Bodleian Library copy, Malone 646(1).   [2] Thomas Elyot, *The Governour*, Chap. I.
[3] C. Middleton, *A Short introduction* . . . , A 3.

133

The *surge* most swoln that *met* him; his bold head
'Bove the contentious waves he kept, and oared
Himself with his good arms in lusty *stroke*
To the shore, that o'er his wave worn basis bowed,
As stooping to relieve him: I not doubt
He came alive to land.   2.1.110

After the plunge, he first *beats* the water. The manual explains to the learner that this "is done swimming upon his backe, and lying straight out with his bodie, the palmes of his hands being downward, and moving up and downe in the water to keepe him up: so may he lift out either one or other of his legges, and beate with it upon the superficies of the water at his pleasure". Doing so, gives Ferdinand time to adjust himself. He then changes his style and stroke by *treading* the water which, as the manual puts it, is "standing bolt up, as it were in the water, and pulling up your feete, and thrusting them downe againe, . . . which have the same force to keepe him that way, which they have to thrust him forwards the other way".

All through he is careful to observe the basic rule, to keep head and mouth above water. A later adapter of Digby's book finds leisure to philosophise on this essential.

> "It may seem an Action very hard and difficult to be performed, for one to swim with his face upwards, and contradictory to our Nature; but it is the most fair, easie and safest way, and most agreeable and suitable to our Nature; whereof the Poet sings,
>
> > Os homini sublime dedit Coelumque:
> > To man God gave looks mixt with Majestie
> > And wil'd him with bold face to view the skie".[1]

Shakespeare's interest in feats of swimming is seen earlier in the swimming contest in *Julius Caesar* which does not come from any historical source but is his own addition. Dramatically it is justified in several ways, and not least because it supports Cassius's argument, and also brings out the stern and resolute side of his character in which both compassion and scorn can mingle.

> For once, upon a raw and gusty day,
> The troubled Tiber chafing with her shores,
> Caesar said to me, 'Dar'st thou, Cassius, now

[1] '*The Compleat Swimmer*: or *The Art of Swimming*: By William Percey, Gent. (1658), p. 22. Ovid *Metamorphoses*, I, 86.

Leap in with me into this angry flood,
And swim to yonder point?' Upon the word,
Accoutred as I was, I plunged in
And bade him follow; so indeed he did.
The torrent roared, as we did buffet it
With lusty sinews, throwing it aside
And stemming it with hearts of controversy.
But ere we could arrive the point proposed,
Caesar cried, 'Help me, Cassius, or I sink!'
                          And this man
Is now become a god, and Cassius is
A wretched creature, and must bend his body
If Caesar carelessly but nod on him.   1.2.99 ff.

Stephano and Trinculo who supply much ludicrous contrast
in *The Tempest* are not minded to be outdone in prowess in swimming.

I swam, ere I could *recover* the shore, five and thirty leagues *off and on*,[1]

is Stephano's boast, and, in wishing to stress that he has overcome adverse conditions, he speaks of himself as a ship on alternate
tacks obliged to make away from shore and then towards it—"off
and on"—but reaching harbour in the end. Trinculo, choosing
to make light of difficulties, talks as if he had the natural skill of a
waterfowl and regards the sea as his native element:

Swum ashore, man, like a duck: I can swim like a duck, I'll be sworn.
                          2.2.129

CLARENCE'S DREAM

In a nightmare dream of teachery, the wonder and terror of the
deep and the horror of drowning are brought together, showing
that another side of the sea, at once fascinating and forbidding,
had a powerful hold on Shakespeare's imagination. The art with
which the tale is told is unusual. Most would require many
words to achieve what Shakespeare has been able to do in com-
pact lines, where language glowing and pictorial is blended with
what is either plain and unadorned, or nautical and technical.

Brief, vivid and partly in seaphrase comes the opening incident:

Methought that I had broken from the Tower,
And was *embarkt to cross* to Burgundy;
And, in my company, my brother Gloster,
Who from my *cabin* tempted me to walk
Upon the *hatches*: thence we looked toward England.
. . . . As we paced along

[1] *Temp.* 3.2.12.

> Upon the *giddy footing* of the *hatches*,
> Methought that Gloster stumbled, and, in falling,
> Struck me, that thought *to stay* him, *overboard*
> Into the *tumbling billows* of the *main*. *R. III* 1.4.8. ff.

It is dramatic in itself and also in wider ways. A dream it may be, but it creates foreboding. The trustfulness and dismay of Clarence and the sudden revelation of Richard's true nature leave in little doubt what is about to be played out. Such treachery breaks the bonds of kinship and is a sacrilege, it also violates the chivalry of the sea, and these breaches open the way to evil that for a time is unbounded.

The wonder of the deep is set against its horror, one being made to heighten the other:

> Methought I saw a thousand fearful wracks
> Ten thousand men that fishes gnawed upon;
> Wedges of gold, great *anchors*, heaps of pearl,
> Inestimable stones, unvalued jewels,
> All scattered in the *bottom of the sea*:
> Some lay in dead men's skulls, and, in those holes
> Where eyes did once inhabit, there were crept,
> As't were in scorn of eyes, reflecting gems,
> That woo'd the slimy *bottom* of the deep,
> And mocked the dead bones that lay scattered by.

The waters close to overwhelm:

> Lord, Lord! methought, what pain it was to *drown*!
> What dreadful noise of waters in mine ears!
> What ugly sights of death within mine eyes.

A question, prompted by natural astonishment, brings a momentary return to the everyday world:

> Had you such leisure in the time of death
> To gaze upon the secrets of the deep?

and this intensifies by contrast the distracted feverish state of mind in which the awful experience of drowning is relived— struggling for breath, passing through degrees of suffocation, striving in desperation to assist death, dying and yet not dying:

> Methought I had, and often did I strive
> To yield the ghost: but still the envious *flood*
> Kept in my soul, and would not let it forth
> To seek the empty vast and wandering air;
> But smothered it within my panting *bulk*,
> Which almost *burst* to *belch* it in the sea.

SEABIRDS AND WATERFOWL

Seabirds, wheeling and circling and filling the air with cries that mingle with the ever-changing sounds of the waves, are inseparable from thoughts of the sea. They have a place in English literature from its earliest beginnings and Old English poetry echoes with the lone cry of the gannet, the plaintive call of the curlew,[1] the scream of the sea-eagle, the shrill, harsh note of the icy winged tern. But in Shakespeare seabirds are few, and their cries are not heard at all.

This may seem surprising when set beside the many landbirds that are mentioned or described: bunting and buzzard, "russet-pated choughs, rising and cawing," crow, cuckoo, daw, dove, eagle, the falcon "towering in her pride", the "temple-haunting martlet", finch, goose, jay, nightingale and "staring owl", parrot, partridge, peacock, pheasant and quail, "the croaking raven," swift, swallow, and starling "taught to speak", sparrow, thrush, tercel, vulture and woodcock and wren "with little quill".

The seabirds and waterfowl that do appear are described as they really are, and not as fancy or false natural history would have them. True to its name is the

> dive-dapper peering through a wave,
> Who, being looked on, ducks as quickly in: *Ven. and Adon.* 86

or the duck "for life that dives".[2] The mallard or drake of the species common wild duck is used as an image of Antony who, "like a doting mallard", follows Cleopatra in her flight (3.10.23).

Cormorants and ospreys were of more than usual interest at the time. Left to themselves, they devour much fish but King James believed that they might be trained to act as fishing hawks and yield up obediently what they had caught. Though he created the office of Master of the Royal Cormorants at Westminster to further the design, his hopes in this, as in much else, were belied.[3]

---

[1] The curlew frequents the sea-shore in winter and the moors in summer.
[2] *Pericles*, 3 Chor. 49.   [3] James E. Harting, *The Ornithology of Shakespeare* (1871), pp. 260–65.

It was therefore both apt and topical to have it said of Coriolanus:

> I think he'll be to Rome
> As is the osprey to the fish, who takes it
> By sovereignty of nature,   4.7.34

and the references to "vanity insatiate cormorant", "cormorant
war" and "cormorant devouring time"[1] were more significant
then than they have since become.

The swan, although its haunts are lakes and meres and rivers,
was looked upon as a seabird in Saxon England, and "the
swan's way" was one of many names given to the sea. Its snow-
white feathers, silver down[2] and black legs are all noted:

> For all the water in the ocean
> Can never turn the swan's black legs to white,
> Although she lave them hourly in the flood   *Tit. And.* 4.2.101

and its protective instincts also:

> So doth the swan her downy cygnets save,
> Keeping them prisoner underneath her wings.   1 *Hen. VI* 5.3.56

Near the water's edge, it builds its "watery nest", and thus
"Britain seems . . . In a great pool a swan's nest" (*Cymb.* 3.4.142).

The ancients ascribed remarkable musical powers to this bird
of Orpheus or Apollo, and when "the death divining swan"
knew its end to be near, it chose to "die in music" (*Oth.* 5.2.246):

> And now this pale swan in her watery nest
> Begins the sad dirge of her certain ending: *Lucrece* 1611.

Musical instruments sound while Bassanio makes his choice of
the caskets in the *Merchant of Venice* so that:

> . . . if he lose, he makes a swan-like end,
> Fading in music.   3.2.44

CREATURES OF THE DEEP

References to creatures of the deep and to various fish are of a
general kind. It is only of the crab, dolphin, oyster and whale
that some fuller knowledge is shown, and even that is not of an
unfamiliar sort. Cod, dogfish, eel, herring, loach, minnow,
mackerel, mussel, pilchard, salmon, shrimp, sprat and tench come
in, but sometimes only as terms of opprobrium. Others are

---

[1] *R. II* 2.1.38; *Troil. and Cres.* 2.2.6; *L.L.L.* 1.1.4.   [2] *Lucrece* 1011.

mentioned when ready for the table, anchovies and sack, conger and fennel, soused gurnet, poor John, stockfish.

The wariness of the carp: "Your bait of falsehood takes this carp of truth;" the odd, sideways and backward motion of the crab: "like a crab, you could go backward;" the dace as a bait for the pike, the gudgeon easily deceived, the trout "caught with tickling", the sportiveness of the dolphin, and how the antics of the porpoise herald a storm, are all noted.[1]

More is made of the whale, its spouting and way of driving small fish before it and devouring them: "they fly or die, like scaled sculls Before the belching whale", and its habit of making for shore and becoming stranded: "his passions, like a whale on ground, Confound themselves with working."[2] Among the ingredients of the witches' cauldron in *Macbeth* are "maw and gulf, Of the ravined salt-sea shark", and Leviathan is used for a sea monster in some heightened figures of speech.[3]

[1] *Ham.* 2.1.63, 2.2.206; 2 *Hen. IV* 3.2.356; *M. of V.* 1.1.102; *T.N.* 2.5.23; *Per.* 2.1.26.
[2] *Troil. and Cres.* 5.5.23; 2 *Hen. IV* 4.4.40; *Macb.* 4.1.23.
[3] *T.G. of V.* 3.2.80; *M.N.D.* 2.1.174; *H. V.* 3.3 26.

SIGNS OF THE WEATHER

The Booke of the Sea Carte has a section entitled "The Mariners Pronostycacion gathered out of Ptolome, Arystotelle, Plini, Virgill and other naturalle philosophers",[1] which contains traditional weather lore like that found in Shakespeare. It is based on the experience of seafarers and also of dwellers inland who know how to read the signs of the sky, and to make forecasts from changes in the sounds and appearance of the sea, or in the force or direction of the wind. The fishermen in *Pericles* are versed in it:

> "Nay, master, said not I as much when I saw the porpus how he bounced and tumbled? . . . a plague on them, they never come but I look to be washed!" 2.1.23

The Booke of the Sea Carte records:

> "The delphyne fysh swemmyng and leapying often tymes above the water, sygnyfyeth great wynd for that quartar"
>
> fol. 70

and Monson observes "there cannot be a truer sign of a storm than whales and porpoises playing upon the water".[2] Foretelling of this sort is made use of in similes in the *Poems*.

> Like a red morn that ever yet betokened
> Wrack to the seaman, tempest to the field,
>   Sorrow to shepherds, woe unto the birds,
>   Gusts and foul flaws to herdmen and to herds. *Ven. and Adon.* 453

> "And the cloudes redd sanguyn appere in the mornying before the sonne rysyng, betokeneth wynd, and yf they be myxte with redd cloudes, yt signyfyeth rayne." fol. 61

Further lore, set down in the same manuscript, underlies the lines:

> And round about her tear distained eye
> Blue circles streamed, like rainbows in the sky:
>   These water-galls in her dim element
>   Foretell new storms to those already spent. *Lucrece*, 1586 ff.

> "Cyrcles of dyverse coloures lyke the rainebow or bryght clouds whych we call wether gales, apperyng abowt the sonne

[1] British Museum, Add. MS. 37,024; fol. 60.   [2] Monson, Vol. V, p. 286.

in the goose summer and wynter, betokeneth vehement frostes and great could wyndes" fol. 70

> As whence the sun'gins his reflection,
> Shipwrecking storms and direful thunders break. *Macbeth* 1.2.24

At the summer solstice the sun is at its greatest distance north, and at the winter solstice at its greatest distance south, of the equator. It appears to stand still, having arrived as it were at its utmost bounds. It then begins to return towards the equator. This return or retrocession or regressive motion was formerly termed "reflection". Unsettled weather, gales and storms are often observed to accompany it.

The forewarning lull before the storm, when the wind drops and the clouds are motionless and a strange stillness spreads, is described in a way that gives a sense of the drama of it.

> But, as we often see, against some storm,
> A silence in the heavens, the rack stand still,
> The bold winds speechless, and the orb below
> As hush as death, anon the dreadful thunder
> Doth rend the region. *Hamlet* 2.2.507

The more frequent signs of bad weather, a lowering sky and ragged low clouds also come in, and take the form of practical instructions:

> the skies look grimly,
> And threaten present blusters . . .
> Make your best haste: and go not
> Too far i' the land: 't is like to be loud weather; *W. Tale* 3.3.3

Trinculo gives a most realistic description of ominous signs overhead and almost makes his hearers share his predicament:

> "Here's neither bush nor shrub to *bear off* any weather, at all, and another storm brewing: I hear it sing i' the wind: yond same black cloud, yond huge one, looks like a foul bombard that would shed his liquor. If it should thunder as it did before, I know not where to hide my head; yond same cloud cannot choose but fall by pailfuls."[1]

He thinks of the approaching storm as something to be fended off if there were any means of doing so, and uses an apt sea term. "Seamen use this word 'bear off', in business belonging to shipping, instead of the word 'thrust off', which to the like sense is most commonly used amongst others."[2]

---

[1] *Temp.* 2.2.18 ff.   [2] Mainwaring, Vol. II, pp. 95–96.

WINDS

The mariner names the "winds of all the corners" by the thirty-two points of the compass, but only those blowing from north, east, south and west and a few others are described in this way by Shakespeare. The rest take their names from a season or month of the year. All are given their proper characteristics.

From the north, "Where shivering cold and sickness pines the clime" (*R. II* 5.1.76), come bleak, sharp, angry winds: " 't is very cold, the wind is northerly" (*Ham.* 5.2.99). Its enlivening effect on the birds of the air is in mind when a messenger is bidden:

> to hie as fast
> As lagging fowls before the northern blast.   *Lucrece* 1334.

The north wind brings tempest:

> the wind was north
> Never was waves nor wind more violent.   *Per.* 4.1.51–59

This is old weather lore and it is found in the fifteenth century *Booke of the Sea Carte*: "The north wynd rysing immedyately after eny south wynde, causith great tempest on the sea."[1] The nor'easter is particularly keen and biting as Aumerle conveniently remembers when explaining their hypocritical leavetaking:

> the north east wind
> Which then blew bitterly against our faces,
> Awaked the sleeping rheum, and so by chance
> Did grace our hollow parting with a tear.   *R. II* 1.4.6

At sea, it has always been an unwelcome wind, and when a man arrives at a naval pay table only to be told that there is nothing for him, he speaks of the rebuff as a "nor'easter".

Though a "prosperous south wind friendly" blows Florizel to Sicily (*W. T.* 5.1.161), the south and the south-west winds are elsewhere associated with "black vapour" and pestilence.[2] The south-west is of ill omen in *Pericles* for when Marina asks artlessly: "Is this wind westerly that blows?", her wouldbe assassin answers in a grim word: "South west" (4.1.50). Apart from this, and the bare mention of a north-north-west wind in *Hamlet*, the westerly wind has no more notice, and the east is heard of only in the fanciful line:

> high Taurus' snow,
> Fanned with the eastern wind,   *M.N.D.* 3.2.141

[1] British Museum, Add. MS. 37, 024, fol. 69.   [2] See Fog, p. 144.

Of the winds of the seasons, "winter's powerful wind" with its "icy fang and churlish chiding",[1] has a song to itself:

Blow, blow, thou winter wind
Thou art not so unkind
As man's ingratitude;
Thy tooth is not so keen,
Because thou art not seen,
Although thy breath be rude.   *A.Y.L.* 2.7.174

"The wind bloweth where it listeth",[2] and Jaques who "must have liberty withal", would have "as large a charter as the wind" (*A.Y.L.* 2.7.48).

The action, movement, direction and force of "winds that sailors rail at" are described in terms that are used at sea. They may *blow in* from every coast, or they may *blow fair from* land.[3] If favourable, they are said to be *at help*, if otherwise, to be *awkward*, and if they veer, to *come about*.[4] Ships *fly* or are *driven before the wind*, flotsam is *carried before the wind*.[5] A wind coming from a certain direction *sits* there: "where sits the wind", "as the wind sits".[6] A *shifted* wind is one that has backed or veered (*K. John*, 4.2.23). If *down*, it has dropped: "if the wind were down, I could drive the boat with my sighs" (*T.G. of V.* 2.3.60). To *lie* is to abate, "The wind is loud, and will not lie" (*Per.* 3.1.48). To *lay* the wind, "rain, to lay this wind" (*T. and C.* 4.4.50), is to cause it to drop or subside.

Whether scientific or imaginative, the words used of the wind by Shakespeare give a sense of its force: "angry, high, rough, rude, raging, splitting, stormy", and also of its mysterious working: "invisible and creeping, viewless, all unseen." They convey, too, its sounds: "howling, loud, piping, warring, scolding, sighing, whistling", and something of its variableness: "adverse, bleak, bold, bounteous, contrarious, cooling, good, inconstant, mutinous." And this drama of nature, in fitful gust, bluster and squall, in brief lull and in calm, is seen to reflect the drama of human life.

FOG

The cooling of damp air is the primary cause of fog. The colder the air, the less moisture it can hold in an invisible state. At sea, fog

---

[1] 3 *Hen. VI* 5.2.15; *A.Y.L.* 2.1.6.
[2] St. John, 3.8. (A.V.).   [3] *M. of V.* 1.1.168; *C. of E.* 4.1.91.   [4] *Ham.* 4.3.46; 2 *Hen. VI*, 3.2.83; *M. of V.* 2.6.64.   [5] *M. of V.* 1.1.14; *Per.* V. Chor. 14; *C. of E.* 1.1.88.   [6] *M. of V.* 1.1.18; *K. Lear* 1.4.113. Also *M. Ado* 2.3.102; *Ham.* 1.3.56, *R. II* 2.2.123.

is most frequent in the late spring and early summer when the temperature of the surface of the water is most likely to be below that of the moist air blowing over it.

When an inland area becomes cooled to a temperature as low as, or lower than, that of the sea, fog may drift in and give rise to that kind of fog, covering both sea and land, which occurs on summer nights. It is described in *Midsummer Night's Dream* and is rightly said to have set in "since the middle summer's spring".

> Therefore the winds, piping to us in vain,
> As in revenge, have sucked up from the sea
> Contagious fogs, which, falling in the land
> Have every pelting river made so proud
> That they have overborne their continents.   2.1.88

This is not a mere flight of fancy. Though poetically worded, it is scientifically sound.

Coming after the cold easterly winds of winter, the warmer southerly winds can produce fog if they blow over a land surface that has been cooled. The south wind thus came to be associated with fog—"foggy south puffing with wind and rain" (*A.Y.L.* 3.5.50). The citizens in *Coriolanus* bring this into their jests, and when one asks:

"Which way do you judge my wit would fly?" he is told, "'t would, sure, southward." "Why that way?" he persists, and is given the answer, "To lose itself in a fog." *Cor.* 2.3.28 ff.

Fog was linked with contagion, with disturbances of the natural order, with curses—"Blasts and fogs upon thee", "The south fog rot him"[1]—and with the doings of witches. They chant together at the end of the opening scene in *Macbeth*:

> Fair is foul, and foul is fair:
> Hover through the fog and filthy air.   1.1.12

Later, Hecate, as she leaves them, calls:

> . . . my little spirit, see,
> Sits in a foggy cloud, and stays for me.   3.5.35

Fog being one of the natural accompaniments of a damp climate, the Constable of France thinks of the English as "a frosty people" and is astonished that they should show such valour:

> where have they this mettle?
> Is not their climate foggy, raw and dull,
> On whom, as in despite, the sun looks pale.   *Hen. V*, 3.5.16

[1] *K. Lear* 1.4.321; *Cymb.* 2.3.136.

CLOUDS

Cloud, as is well known, is formed by the condensation of water vapour in the atmosphere at a height above the earth's surface. The main formations are classified as cirrus, cumulus, nimbus and stratus, but these scientific terms by themselves do not enable everyone to build up a picture of what is being described or defined, and the scientist may therefore use other words that make this possible—woolpack, cauliflower, mackerel, feathery, fibrous, fleecy, heaped, patchy. The different forms may be spoken of as bands, ripples, streaks, tufts or wisps.

This kind of description, aiming at telling what various types of cloud look like, is what is found in Shakespeare, and the words he applies to them may be either realistic or fanciful or a blend of both—black, curled, dark, lazy-pacing, racking, severing; dying, suspicious, threatening, weeping.

He gives a vivid and remarkable picture of ragged cumulus in which the different parts show constant change:

> Sometime we see a cloud that's dragonish;
> A vapour sometime like a bear or lion,
> A tower'd citadel, a pendant rock,
> A forked mountain, or blue promontory
> With trees upon't, that nod unto the world,
> And mock our eyes with air: thou hast seen these signs;
> They are black vesper's pageants.
> That which is now a horse, even with a thought
> The rack dislimns and makes it indistinct
> As water is in water.   *Ant. and Cleo.* 4.14.2 ff.

Calphurnia talks of "most horrid sights seen by the watch":

> Fierce fiery warriors fought upon the clouds
> In ranks and squadrons and right form of war,
> Which drizzled blood upon the Capitol;   *Julius Caesar*, 2.2.19.

without knowing that these seeming portents can be accounted for scientifically. Rain of a red colour, "blood rain", which leaves a red stain on the ground, occurs when the raindrops contain small particles of dust which have been carried from sandy regions by currents in the upper air.

"When clouds are seen, wise men put on their cloaks", but

"every cloud engenders not a storm",[1] and some may pass without a shower through the various effects of ascending and descending currents of warm or cool air.

> But when a black-faced cloud the world doth threat,
> In his dim mist the aspiring mountains hiding,
> From earth's dark womb some gentle gust doth get,
> Which blows these pitchy vapours from their biding
> Hindering their present fall by this dividing. *Lucrece* 547

Stratified cloud, formed at night, may disappear during the morning especially in summer, "to the brightest beams, distracted clouds give way", because the heat of the sun's rays causes them to evaporate, the "very beams will dry those vapours up".[2]

Cloud and vapour driving across the sun is a familiar and unwelcome sight, and Shakespeare describes not only what takes place, but the feelings with which it may be watched:

> Full many a glorious morning have I seen
> Flatter the mountain-tops with sovereign eye,
> Kissing with golden face the meadows green,
> Gilding pale streams with heavenly alchemy;
> Anon permit the basest clouds to ride
> With ugly rack on his celestial face,
> And from the forlorn world his visage hide,
> Stealing unseen to west with this disgrace:
> Even so my sun one early morn did shine
> With all triumphant splendour on my brow;
> But, out, alack! he was but one hour mine,
> The region cloud hath maskt him from me now. *Sonnet 33*

At other times, a dark veil of thin altostratus may cover the sky and appear to

> stain the sun with fog, as sometime clouds
> When they do hug him in their melting bosoms. *Tit. And.* 3.1.213

In the path of a flash of lightning, intense heating causes the air to expand very rapidly, and with almost explosive violence, and the sound waves thus set up are heard "as thunder when the clouds in autumn crack" (*T. of S.* 1.2.96).

[1] *R. III* 2.3.32; 3 *Hen. VI* 5.3.13.   [2] *All's W.* 5.3.35; 3 *Hen. VI* 5.3.12.

EPILOGUE

The novelist can expand, describe, discuss and explain, the dramatist must compress. Had Shakespeare been writing a series of novels, his knowledge of navigation, seamanship, strategy and seaphrase could have been fully disclosed. But the plays allow him scope for no more than a revealing outline or summary of it. Even from this, however, it is not difficult to see how much more he must have known. What appears in *Henry VI* gives the impression of one who has recently left the sea and whose thoughts keep turning to it. This goes on throughout the early plays and is also seen in the poems and sonnets. It continues in the plays of the second period where none of the references should be underestimated, brief and detached as some may be. Then, in the great tragedies, seafaring has a new importance and gives rise to unique scenes and incidents in *Hamlet*, *Othello* and *Antony and Cleopatra*. In the last plays, all that has gone before reappears with remarkable freshness and much is added, for the themes make it possible to bring in wider knowledge of seamanship, ceremony, the duties of officers, the ways of seamen and also of storm and tempest.

How did Shakespeare come to know "an art beyond most of others, not to be snatched at, at idle times and on the bye, but rather requiring so full a taking up of a man in the learning of it; as for the time nothing else is to be looked after"[1]?

Much has been written about the gap in what is known of Shakespeare's life and, despite attempts to suggest how the years 1584–90 may have been passed, they cannot be accounted for satisfactorily. One thing can be taken as certain, it was during this period that Shakespeare came to know the sea and the navy. The times were dangerous and stirring. Defence measures against Spain began in earnest in 1583 and war was declared in 1585. There were musters and levies in all the counties, and men from shires inland were drafted to reinforce levies in counties bordering on the sea. Lists of the ships that were fitted out or in reserve are remarkably complete and contain much detail about equipment,

[1] Boteler, p. 3.

victualling and the numbers of men borne, but the muster rolls
name only senior officers and captains. The state papers reveal
nothing that would help in discovering where Shakespeare may
have been or in what ships he might have served. Some list,
despatch or memorandum may yet bring more to light, but until
that happens, evidence of another kind must be relied on. This
is to be found in the extent and accuracy of his nautical knowledge
which is that of one familiar with the duties of an officer. He
could have held one of the temporary commissions created during
the emergency. His abilities and the influence of his mother's
family which was of standing would make this probable. Some
general learning was required for these commissions and men
were not chosen "merely for their marinership". His rank would
most likely be that of corporal;[1] it was not a non-commissioned
rank then, as it is today. He may have been promoted or been
considered for promotion to lieutenant[2] for his interest in the rank,
his knowledge of the duties that belong to it and of the methods
of election to it, can hardly be without significance. But such
matters cannot be determined from records that are known.

An outstanding career may sometimes be taken as a guide to
what might happen in a lesser way to others, and William
Monson's is of particular interest here. His parents had sent him
to Balliol College, Oxford, but study was less to his mind than
defiance of Spain and he ran away to sea. "I was a youth of
sixteen years of age, and so inclined to see the world abroad that,
without the knowledge of father or mother I put myself into an
action by sea . . . and was an actor at the taking of the first
Spanish prize."[3] Within two years, he found himself in command
of an armed vessel authorised by the crown to seize the subjects
and goods of the King of Spain. Against the Armada he served as
a volunteer, braving storm and gunfire in a slight but nimble
vessel, the Queen's pinnace *Charles*. Ill health kept him ashore
in 1590, but early in the following year he was at sea again, only
to be taken and held in the castle at Lisbon till 1592. A spell
ashore followed his release and, returning to Oxford which he had
forsaken seven years before, he became an M.A. in 1594. The
summer of 1597 saw him Essex's flag captain in command of the
Rainbow, "the most rolling and laboursome ship in England",

---

[1] See p. 56. A rank in the Royal Marines now but no longer in the Navy.
   See pp. 54–55
[3] Monson, Vol. V, pp. 173–74. (His dates are c. 1568–1643.)

and his services were rewarded with a knighthood. In the great mobilisation of 1599, he commanded the *Defiance*, and by 1604 he was Admiral of the Narrow Seas. His eventful life drew to a quiet close in the reign of King Charles the First. He died at the age of seventy-five and was buried with honour at St. Martin's-in-the-Fields. The writings which he left on the navy as he had known it under three monarchs remain of great interest and value.

"One man in his time plays many parts", and, in excitements and abrupt changes such as those that crowded Monson's life, Shakespeare may have shared for a few years.

"The sea language is not soon learned, much less understood, being only proper to him that has served his apprenticeship."[1]

Shakespeare is the first to bring a wide range of sea terms into drama and poetry. He is at ease in an idiom unknown to most and his scope and precision can be adequately illustrated only in an analytical glossary.

His use of sea language is always appropriate, and will be found so even where occasionally it may appear to be otherwise at first sight. The nautical rhetoric of Queen Margaret in *Henry VI*, with its shrouds, tacklings, anchors, cables, hatches, helm, masts and sails, has been thought strange in a queen, a lapse perhaps while Shakespeare is finding his way in early work. But there are sound reasons for it. Margaret is being presented as a patriot queen, undaunted in the face of her enemies. England is her adopted land, she identifies herself wholly with it, and her talk of the sea and ships gives emphasis to that. It has also to be remembered that Queen Elizabeth herself could have made nautical speeches very much of this kind with little effort. The despatches, inventories of prizes, surveys of ships, details of damage, charges for grounding, ransacking, dubbing and caulking which poured in to her were filled with sea terms and technical language, and jottings in her own hand on the back of such documents show that she did more than glance at them. Howard, Drake and Raleigh when they wrote to her never tried to avoid nautical terms, nor did they presume to simplify them. To the Elizabethans, Margaret's speeches would make a strong appeal and would seem most fitting for an island queen.

Monson, Vol. III, p. 434.

More than a thousand years have gone by since Alfred the Great founded his navy and launched its victorious Long Ships, and each passing century has added new glories to a sea tradition that has gathered into it and fostered and enriched much that is greatest in English life. Shakespeare knew and felt its power and has paid his tribute.

HARK, DO YOU HEAR THE SEA?
King Lear 4.6.4.

APPENDIX I

A TOMB BY THE SEA SHORE

"Lie where the light foam of the sea may beat
Thy grave stone daily." *Timon of Athens*, 4.3.380

Timon decides that "his everlasting mansion" shall be:

Upon the beached verge of the salt flood,
Who once a day with his embossed froth
The turbulent surge shall cover. 5.1.214

Alienated from mankind, he scorns human tears, "droplets . . .
from niggard nature" and, "entombed upon the very hem o' the
sea", proudly commands an unceasing tribute from the vast
ocean:

Though thou abhorr'dst in us our human griefs,
Scorn'dst our brains' flow and those our droplets which
From niggard nature fall, yet rich conceit
Taught thee to make vast Neptune weep for aye
On thy low grave, on faults forgiven. 5.4.75

Plutarch tells that Timon died in the city of Hales and that he
was buried by the seaside. But Shakespeare makes this choice
of a last resting place the act of one who has turned against men
for ever because of their heartlessness and ingratitude, and he
surrounds it with a dignity that is sombre, grave and majestic.

A BLESSING FOR ONE BORN AT SEA IN A STORM

Here is a thing too young for such a place,
Who, if it had conceit, would die, as I
Am like to do. *Pericles* 3.1.15

When the tempest is raging as though it would never be stilled,
and Pericles can do no more than entreat:

Yet for the love
Of this poor infant, this fresh-new seafarer
I would it would be quiet 3.1.40

he collects himself to give his blessing to the newborn Marina:

> Now, mild may be thy life!
> For a more blusterous birth had never babe;
> Quiet and gentle thy conditions! for
> Thou are the rudeliest welcome to this world
> That e'er was prince's child. Happy what follows!
> Thou hast as chiding a nativity
> As fire, air, water, earth, and heaven can make,
> To herald thee from the womb. Poor inch of nature!
> Even at the first thy loss is more than can
> Thy portage quit, with all thou canst find here.
> Now the good gods throw their best eyes upon't!   3.1.27 ff.

APPENDIX II

The Boatswain is addressed, quite unjustifiably, as "bawling, blasphemous, uncharitable dog" by Sebastian who is Antonio's accomplice in villainy. Later, Gonzalo hails him with:

> Now, blasphemy,
> That swearest grace o'erboard, not an oath on shore?
> Hast thou no mouth by land? 5.1.218

He is certainly not heard infringing the naval regulations on swearing at any point in the drama. These were very strict:

> You shall take especial care that God be not blasphemed in your ship, but that after admonition given, if the offenders do not reform themselves, you shall cause them of the meaner sort to be ducked at yard-arm, and the better sort to be fined out of their adventure. By which course if no amendment be found, you shall acquaint me withal, delivering me the names of the offenders. For if it be threatened in the Scriptures that the curse shall not depart from the house of the swearer, much less shall it depart from the ship of the swearer.[1]

Raleigh shared in the concern about swearing grace overboard, for he placed this traditional order second in the list of instructions issued at Plymouth when he set out on his last expedition in May 1617.

Oaths were prohibited on the stage by the "Act to Restraine Abuses of Players" of 1606, and Shakespeare in 1611 would be unlikely to put in what he knew would have to be taken out, or if he did, would hardly fail afterwards to remove remarks bearing on what was no longer there. A further difficulty is that it is the business of the Boatswain to enforce the law, not to break it. He is shown carrying out all his duties in a way that leaves nothing to be desired, and it would be strange if he fell short in this. The charges are levelled at him by courtiers whom he has had to rebuke. They are resentful. Even Gonzalo says of him that he will be hanged one day. The others are given to indiscriminate abuse, and this may be another instance of it, serving to expose the prejudices and unreasonableness of landsmen.

[1] *Fighting Instructions*, pp. 36–37.

APPENDIX III

A NAVIGATIONAL SONNET

Let me not to the *marriage* of *true* minds
Admit impediments. Love is not love
Which *alters* when it *alteration* finds,
Or *bends* with the *remover to remove*:
Oh no! it is an ever-*fixed mark*,
That looks on *tempests*, and is never *shaken*;
It is *the star* to every *wandering bark*,
Whose worth's unknown, although his *height* be *taken*.
Love's not Time's fool, though rosy lips and cheeks
Within his bending sickle's compass come;
Love *alters* not with his brief *hours and weeks*,
But *bears it out* even to the edge of doom
If this be *error*, and upon me *prov'd*,
I never writ, nor no man ever lov'd.   *Sonnet 116*

In almost every line of this sonnet, some words or phrases are used in a navigational sense as well as in the ordinary way. They follow in an order that links together true direction, alteration of course, taking latitude and meeting dangers. These are all of chief importance in navigation, and they illustrate the idea on which the thought of the poem turns.

The double thread is kept running skilfully, and so much is implied that it would be difficult to render this as a sonnet, line for line, into another tongue. The words could not be translated as they stand for the twofold meaning would have to be brought out in a paraphrase. This would add to the length of the original, and change the whole tone.

The theme is constancy, "the marriage of true minds". In navigation, true north must be found if true direction and true bearings are to be known. It is the basis of all calculation of this kind. In determining it, the age-long aid of the navigator is the Pole star, the North star, the Lodestar. "It is the star to every wandering bark",

Of whose true-fixed and resting quality
There is no fellow in the firmament.
                    Julius Caesar 3.1.60

The description of the bark as *wandering* is drawn from the distinction between the fixed and the wandering stars. Ships at sea can tell where they are from the true altitude of the Pole star because this is also the latitude of the place from which the observation is made. For this reason, *height* was the usual word for latitude.

Another emblem of constancy is the sea-mark, the "ever-fixed mark", withstanding the ebb and flow all around and remaining unshaken by tempest.

Though *time, compass, alter* and *hours* are used first of all in the ordinary sense, it must not be overlooked that they have navigational meanings connected with calculations for finding direction and position. These have a further bearing on the theme.

Alter and *alteration* are navigational terms. It is incorrect to use "change" when speaking of alterations of course. To *bear out* is to hold out or to weather a storm. It is said of the storm-tossed fleet in *Othello*.

> "It is impossible they bear it out."

Error in navigation comes under several headings, error in observed altitude, compass error and others. Its use in the closing couplet is in keeping with what has gone before.

Bend and *shake* are terms in seamanship, and "marry the falls" is one of the orders in hoisting a sea-boat. The *falls* are held together, side by side, and handled as one. These are fainter parallels, but they add to the associations of the sea and of the art of navigation which shape and reinforce the thought all through.

INDEX

ACHILLES, 74
Admiral, 53, 60, 69, 99
Adriana, 6
Agamemnon, 74
Agincourt, 53, 76
Aground, 37
A-hold, 38
Ajax, 64
Aleppo, 58
Alfred the Great, 150
Algiers, 49
Almanac, 90, 91
Alonso, 45, 54, 58, 59, 72
"Alter", 63, 64
America, 100
American Neptune, The, 38
Anchor, 103, 104
Anchorage, 103, 108
Andrew, 112, 113; *see also St. Andrew* (ship)
Andrew, Sir, 92
Andrews, Kenneth R., 26
Annales of England, 23
Antoniad, 53
Antonio, *M. of V.*, 83; *T. Night*, 45, 50–54, 97; *Temp.*, 65, 153
Antony, Mark, 13–19, 22, 94, 107, 137, 145
Antwerp, 104
Apollo, 138
Arber Edward, xv, 8, 130, 131, 132
Argosy, 22, 82, 99
Ariel, 39, 58, 87, 111
Arion, 45
Aristotle, 77
Ark Royal, 55
Armada (Spanish), xi, xiii, 7, 9, 17, 28, 55, 98, 117, 148
Armado, 90, 100, 119
Art of Navigation in England, xiv
Arte of Shooting, 117
Arthur, Prince, 67
Arviragus, 64
Ashley, Antony, xiv

Astrolabe, xiii
Astronomy, xiii, 93–95
Atkinson, Thos., 58
Augustus Caesar, 13–17, 60
Aumerle, 142
Ayde (ship), 123
Azores, 35

Bank, 82–85
Banquet, 18, 23
Bardolph, 68, 69, 84, 121, 122
Barents, William, 92
Barge, 18–21, 99, 108, 109, 111
Bargulus, 5
Bark, 83, 102
Barlow, William, 89
Basilisk, 119, 120
Bassanio, 83, 138
"Bawbling", 52
Beacon, 78, 79, 82
Beak, 105
Bear, Great, 93, 94, 95
Bear, Little, 90, 93, 94
"Bear off", 141
"Bear up", 56, 107
Beatrice, 94
Beazley, C. R., 35
Becalm, 114, 115
Belarius, 87
Benedick, 94
Bertram, 122
Best, George, 89
Bilboes, 122
Birds (land), 137
Biscuit, 64
Blaeu, W. J., 83
Blavet, 28
Blessing . . . at sea, 151, 152
"Blood rain", 144
Blundeville, Thos., xiv; *Exercises*, xiv, 93
Boarding, 48, 50, 51, 69, 117
Boat, 44, 45, 102
Boatswain, 37, 38, 41, 42, 54, 56, 57, 58–60, 65, 66, 108, 153

Booke of the Sea Carte, The, 140, 141, 142

Boteler, Nathaniel, *Dialogues,* 10, 14–25, 37, 38, 53, 55, 56, 57, 58, 60, 67, 68, 69, 71, 72, 80, 81, 98, 99, 101, 103, 104, 105, 108, 111, 113, 115, 122, 125, 126

Bourne, William, 117

Bowline, 38, 41, 115

Bowsprit, 110, 111

Boys, 66, 67

Brabantio, 104

Brest, 28

Bridgewater, 50

Briefe and a true Discourse (Marbeck's), 66

Bristol, xv, (Channel), 49

Britain's Buss, 131

Brittany, 28, 114

Broadside, 119

Brutus, 95

Buckingham, Duke of, 84, 85

Bulk, 52

Bunt, 115

Buoy, 78, 79, 82

Buoyancy, 44, 45

Burgundy, Duke of, 118

Buss, 100, 101

Butt, 46, 101

"Buzz", 64

Cabin, 105

Cable, 103, 104

Cade, Jack, 119

Cadiz, 15, 28, 51, 66, 113

Caesar, *see* Augustus, Julius

Calais Roads, 104

Calculations, 123

Calendar, 89, 90, 91

Caliban, 56, 65, 71, 72, 84

Calibre, 121

Caliver, 121

Calm, 114, 115

Calphurnia, 145

Cambridge, 35

Camillo, 73

Cannon, 118–20

Canvas, 113; "full canvas", 114

Canvas-climber, 64

Captain, 3, 5, 53, 54, 57

Carcass, 46, 83, 97, 101

Card (sea-card), 89

Carew, George, Lord, 49

Carrack, 100

Carriage (guns), 118

Cartography, xiv

Casca, 43, 95

Cassio, 11, 55, 115, 119

Cassius, 96, 134, 135

Cast adrift, 46

Castaways, 45

Cavendish, Henry, 91

Ceremony, 10, 18–27, 60

Certain errors—(Wright), 35, 92

Chain of command, 58

Channel, English, 3, 4, 83 (the Narrow Seas), 97

Charles I, 129, 149

Charles II, xvi, 68

Charles' Wain, 95

Chatham, 113

Chough, 121, 128

Cinna, 95

Clap, 106, "Clap on", 69, 115

Clarence, 105, 106, 135, 136

Claudius, King of Denmark, 32, 119, 120

Cleopatra, 14–16, 94, 99, 107, 108, 109, 111, 114, 115, 137

Clouds, 145, 146

Cock-boat, 4, 5, 98, 99

Cockle, 101

Colours, 20–21

Command, *see* Leadership

Commissions, 51, 54, 69, 147

Compass, 89, 90, 142

Compleat Swimmer, The, 134

Constable of France, 144

Continental Shelf, 86

Convoys, 3

Copernicus, 94

Copland, Robert, 86

Corbett, Julian S., 42

Coriolanus, 78, 108, 109, 138

Cormorant, 137, 138

Cornwall, 28

Corporal, 54, 56, 148

Cotton, Joseph, 78

Council (naval), 8

Course (sail), 38, 115, (direction), 63, 64

Cowley, Abraham, xvi

Crab, 138, 139

Crare, 87, 101

Cromwell, Thomas, 84

Culverin, 119, 120

Cumberland, Earl of, 29, 35
Current, 77
"Cut and run", 104
Cyprus, 7, 107

Dangers to navigation, 82–85
Dardan, 125
Dartmouth, 100
Dauphin, 83
Davis, John, 92, 123
De Arte Natandi, 133
Decius, 95
Deck, terms used with, 105
Dee, John, 130
Defeat of the Spanish Armada, 8, 13, 17,
    30, 55, 57, 66, 117
Defence of the Realme, 1, 3
Defiance, 149
Delay, 102
Demicannon, 119, 120
De Motibus Stellae Martis, 94
Denmark, 23, 48
Deptford, xvi, 78
Desdemona, 11, 12, 100, 101, 119
Dials, 90–91
Digby, Everard, 133
Dive-dapper, 137
"Dock", 113
Dogs, 72
Dolphin, 45, 133, 138, 139, 140
Donne, John, 36
Douglas, Earl of, 121
Dover cliff, 98, 127–128
Downs, The, 4, 103
Drake, Sir Francis, xiii, xiv, xvi, 11,
    13, 14, 20, 27, 40, 42, 50, 53, 90, 149
Drake and the Tudor Navy, 42
"Driving", 45
Dromio, 100
Drowning, 136
Drunkenness, 65

Eastward Ho, 36
Ebb, 73
Eddy, 75
Edgar, 87, 127, 128
Edmund, 91, 96
Edward VI, 129
Effingham, Lord Charles Howard of,
    xiv, 14, 15, 28, 30, 49, 54–56, 66,
    117, 149
Egyptian ships, 17

Elizabeth, Queen, xi, xvi, 13, 29, 47,
    113, 129, 149
Elizabeth, consort of Edward IV, 109
Elsinore, 23
Elyot, Thos., 133
Embarking, 32, 33
England's Exchequer, 50
England's Way to Win Wealth, 131
English Garner, An, xv, 8, 130, 131, 132
English Privateering Voyages, 26
Enobarbus, 19, 22, 68, 105, 109
Ensigns, 20, 21, 22
Escott, George, 50
Essex, Earl of, 15, 28, 31, 36, 90, 113,
    148
Euxine, 77
Expedition, 102
Exploration, 3

Fabian, 92
Falcon, 119
Falconet, 119
Falstaff, 53, 68, 69, 84, 98, 100, 106,
    108, 119, 121, 122
Fathom, 86, 87
Fathom line, 86
Fenner, Sir Thos., 17
Ferdinand, 45, 133, 134
Ferris, Richard, xv
Fighting Instructions, 37, 61, 65, 68, 119,
    153
Fights, 69
Fireships, 104
First sight of land, 34
Fish, 138, 139
Fish days, 130
Fishermen, 44, 129–32, 140
Fixed stars, 94
Flags, uses of, 20, 21, 22, 26
Flanders, 97
Flat, 83
Flaw, 78, 79
Fleet, Royal, 30
Fleet instructions, 37, 69, 119
Flood, 73–77
Flores, 112
Florizel, 33, 142
Fly (compass), 89
Fog, 143, 144
Ford, Mrs., 69, 106, 121
Foresail, 38, 39
France, 3, 74
Frobisher, Martin, 63, 76, 123

Galley, xvi, 7, 17, 28, 97, 104
Gallias, 98
Gaunt, John of, 1
General, 10, 15, 53, 60
Gentleman, Tobias, 131
Geography, xiii
Geometry, xiii
Gibraltar, 97
"Give fire", 69, 118, 119
Glass, *see* Hour-glass
Globes, 91–92
Glossaries (nautical), xiii, 39
Gloster, Richard of, 22, 105
Golden Hind, xvi
Golden Lion, 23
Gondola, 101
Gondolier, 101
Gonzalo, 59, 65, 104, 153
Goodman, Godfrey, 23
Goodwin sands, 83, 97
Governour, The, 133
Grappling, 48, 50, 117
Gravelines, 55
Gravesend, 23, 70
Grenville, Sir Richard, 112
Gresham, Sir Thomas, xiii; College, xiii, xiv
Ground, 86–88
Guards, The, 90, 93, 94
Gun, 10, 20, 23, 25, 56, 121
Gunner, 56
Gunnery, 117–22
Gunner's terms, 118 ff.
Gunpowder, 119

Hagthorpe, John, 50
Hakluyt, Richard, xiii, xiv; *Principal Navigations*, xiii, xiv, xv, 45, 46, 76
Hal, Prince, 22, 73
Hale (haul), 42, 110
Hales, 151
Hall's *Chronicle*, 4
Hamlet, 23, 33, 47, 48, 64, 105, 120–123
Hardy, Thomas M., 58
Harting, James, 137
Hastings, Lord, 65
Hatches, 69, 105, 106, 107, 136
Hawkins, Sir Richard, 10
Hecate, 144
Height (latitude), 94
Helena, 122
Helicanus, 21

Hellespont, 11, 77
Helm, 38, 56, 107
Henry IV, 67
Henry V, 30, 31, 120, 121
Henry VI, 99
Henry VIII, 106, 117
Hill, Andrew, xv
Historical MSS. Commission, 113
Hitchcock, Robert, 130
Hold, 106
Holland, Philemon, 77
Hood, Thomas, xiii
Horatio, 63, 121, 123
Hotspur, 86, 120, 121
Hour-glass, 81, 91
Howard, *see* Effingham and Nottingham
Hoy, 101
Hudson, Henry, 46
Hues, Robert, 91
Hulk, 100
Hull, 106, 107
Hulling, 106
Humanitarianism, 115
Hurricano, 126

Iago, 55, 68, 100, 104, 115
Icicle, 92
Imogen, 103, 110
Indies, 51, 28, 69, 92, 126
Invasion, 28
Inventories, 123, 149
Isabel, Queen of France, 120
Islands Voyage, 113

James I, xii, 23, 47, 48, 49, 129, 137
Jaques, 64, 90, 143
Jessica, 101
Joan of Arc, 118
John, King, 74, 109, 115
Jonah, 36
Julia, 32
Julius Caesar, 43
Jury mast, 44, 111
Justice, Lord Chief, 22

Keel, 107
Kent, 4
Kepler, John, 94
Knell, 25
Knyvett, Sir H., 1, 3

Laertes, 32, 123
La Rochelle, 113

Last sight of shore, 33, 34
Laughton, J. L., 8
Law and Custom of the Sea, 47, 51
Lawrence, Friar, 119
"Lay aboard", 4
"Lay off", 39
Leadership, 14–17
Leigh in Essex, 49
Lear, 43
Lepidus, 19
Leviathan, 139
Lieutenant, 4, 5, 9, 54–56, 98, 148
Lighthouse, 79
Light of Navigation, 83
Linstock, 118
Lizard, 86
Lisbon, 112, 148
Lloyd, Christopher, 9
"Loath-to-Depart", 19, 20
London, xi, xii, xiii, xv, 28, 49, 82
Lodestar, 93
London Bridge, 75, 82
Long-boat, 4, 5, 98
Long Ships, 150
"Loof", 10, 56, 115
Lorenzo, 101
Lundy, 49
Lysimachus, 21

Macbeth, 84
Madre de Dios, 100
Mainmast, 40, 57, 110
Maintop, 100
Mainwaring, Sir H., xii; *Works*, xii,
　　36, 38, 52, 57, 70, 75, 84, 86, 89,
　　103, 104–7, 110, 115, 123, 141
Mallard, 137
Malvolio, 74
Manoeuvres, 37, 38, 39, 41
Maps, 82, 92; *Map of the World*, xv, 92
Marbeck, Roger, 66 (Account of
　　Howard)
Margaret, Queen, 22, 34, 84, 103, 106,
　　107, 149
Maria, 61, 106, 114
Marina, 41, 48, 142
Mariner's Mirror, 19
Mariners Mirrour, xiv, 82
Maritime supremacy, 13
Markham, A. H., 92
Markham C. R., 10, 91
Mars, 94
Marsden, R. G., 47

Marvell, Andrew, 111
Mast, 38, 41, 44, 109, 110, 111
Master, 3, 4, 10, 37, 41, 42, 54, 56,
　　57–58, 80
Master-at-arms, 59
Master gunner, 118
Master's mate, 4, 37, 80
Mathematics, 55, 123
Medina Sidonia, 117
Mediterranean, 49, 97
Memoir on the Origin of Trinity House, 78
Menas, 19, 49, 104
Menecrates, 49
Mercator, 92
Merchant ships, 3, 99, 100
Middleton, Christofer, 133, 134
Minion, 119
Miranda, 43, 46, 101
Mizzen, 110
Mobilisations, 28, 29, 149
Molyneux, Emery, xiv, 91
Monson, Sir William, xi, xii, 23, 49,
　　112, 113, 140, 148, 149; *Naval
　　Tracts*, xi, 4, 15, 23, 28, 29, 35, 48,
　　49, 50, 52, 53, 54, 55, 57, 58, 60, 61,
　　63, 80, 81, 97, 113, 117, 118, 140,
　　148, 149
Montgomery, John, 82, 98
Moon and tide, 73
Mortarpiece, 120
Moth, 119
Murdering piece, 120
Musket, 122
Music, power of, 62
Muster rolls, 147, 148
Mutines, 122
Mytelene, 20, 21

Napier, John, Baron Merchiston, 123;
　　Mirifici Logarithmorum, 123
Naval Miscellany, The, 9
Navigation, xii, xiii, 3, 39, 55, 82, 123;
　　instruments, 89–92
Navigator's Supply, The, 89
Navy Royal, xi
Nell, 100
Nelson, Horatio (Admiral) 13, 14, 58,
　　66
Nestor, 102
New England, 38
Newton, Sir Izaac, 73
Nicolas, N. H., 14
Norfolk, Duke of, 84

Norman, Robert, xiii
North, 92, 142
North Star, 93, 94
Northumberland, Earl of, 43
Nottingham, Earl of, see Effingham
Novaya Zemlya, 92
Nym Corporal, 56

Oar, 111
Oaths, 153
"Off and on", 135
Officer of the Watch, 19
Olivia, 61, 74
Ooze, 87, 88, 113
Ophelia, 32
Oppenheim, M., xi
Ordnance, English, excellence of, 117, 118
Orleans, 118
Ornithology of Shakespeare, The, 137
Orpheus, 138
Osprey, 137, 138
Osric, 122, 123
Othello, 7–12, 42, 55, 68, 77, 80, 97, 100, 104, 108, 119
Ovid, 134
Oxford, xiii, xvi, 66, 91, 148
Oyster, 138

Page, Mrs., 69
Patriotism, 1, 2
Pepys, Samuel, xvi
Penzance, 28
Percey, W., The Compleat Swimmer, 134
Percy, Henry (Hotspur), 120, 121;
    Lady Percy, 120
Perdita, 33
Pericles, 20, 21, 24–27, 40, 41, 45, 54, 66, 105, 110, 129, 131, 151, 152
Perrin, W. G., 10
Persia, 5
Petar(d), 120
Petruchio, 120
Physician, 61–62
Pillage, 71, 72
Pilot, 79–81
Pilot's "charge", 80
Pink, 69, 70, 101
Pinnace, 4, 5, 69, 98, 148
Pirates, xv, 4, 5, 47–52, 69, 70, 79, 107
Pistol, 121
Pistol, Ancient, 68–70, 118, 121
"Play the men", 54

Pliny, 77
Plough(Ursa Major), 93, 94, 95
Plummet, 86–88
Plutarch, 13, 15, 17, 18, 19, 49, 151
Plymouth, xv, 10, 153
Point blank, 119
Point (of compass), 89, 142
Politic Plat, A., 130, 131
Pole star, 93, 94
Polonius, 32, 64
Pompey, 18, 19, 60, 104, 109
Pontic, 11, 77
Poop, 60, 69, 107
Porpoise, 139, 140
Portsmouth, 111, 113
Portugal, 86, 100
Posthumus, 103, 105
Powder, see Gunpowder
Privateers, 50–52, 69
Privy-Council, 14
Proclamation of 1603, 51
Prognostication, 91
Promontories, 127, 128
Propontic, 11, 77
Prospero, 39, 46, 50, 58, 71, 72, 75, 84, 88, 101, 108, 114
Proteus, 32
Ptolemy, 94
Purchas His Pilgrimes, 9, 40, 42
Purfleet, 82
Putting to sea, 30–34

Queenborough, 70
Queen's Foreland, 76
Quickly Mrs., 69

Ragozine, 48
Rain (blood), 145
Rainbow, 148
Raleigh, Sir Walter, 113, 117, 149, 153
Recoil, 119
"Reflection", 141
Repulse, 113
Revenge, 112
Rhodes, 8
Ribs, 112, 113
Richard III, 65; see also Gloster
Richmond, 53, 107, 114
Rigging, 108
Rocks, 82–85
Roderigo, 104

Romeo, 80, 81, 110, 118, 119
Room, 105; *see also* sea-room
Rope, 109, 110
Rosalind, 86, 101
Royal Exchange, xiii
Royal Marines, 68
Royal Navy, xi, xiii, 1, 3–31, 60, 64, 147, 148
Rudder, 107
Rule of the North Star, 94
Rutter of the Sea, 86

Safeguard of Sailers, The, xiii
Sails, 109, 113–16
Sailing terms, 114, 115
Sailors, 8, 19–21, 24, 25, 57, 59, 68–70
Saker, 119
Salkeld Thomas (pirate), 49, 50
Salutes, 10, 19, 20, 22, 23
Sandbank, 82–85
Saturn, 91
Say, Lord, 119
Scheldt, 104
Sea and sky, 42, 43
Sea birds, 137, 138
Sea burial, 24, 25
Sea-card, 89
Sea defeat, 13–17
"Sea fire", 39, 40
Sea Grammar, A, 54
Seagull, Captain, 36
Seaman's Dictionary (Nomenclator Navalis), xii
Seamanship, xii, 3, 37, 38, 39, 114
Seaman's Secrets, The, 123
Seamark, 78, 79
Seamen (see sailors), 37, 39, 41, 42, 63–66
Sea room, 38, 41
Sea soldiers, 68–70
Sea terms (accurate use of), *see* Shakespeare
Sebastian, 153
Seiches, 125
Seneca, 4
Sennet, 18
Serpentine, 119
Shakespeare, xi, xii; interest in sea and navy xii; knowledge of rank of lieutenant, 4–9, 54–56; missing years and sea service, possible rank, 147–149; patriotism, 1, 2; sea terms, xiii, 5, 6, 17, 31,

Shakespeare (*contd.*)
36, 39, 42, 46, 69, 77, 83, 86, 87 101, 114, 135, 143, 149
Plays:
All's Well, 81, 122, 146
Antony and Cleopatra, 14–20, 22, 49, 53, 60, 73, 74, 94, 97, 99, 104, 105, 107, 109, 111, 114, 115, 116, 137, 145
As You Like It, 86, 90, 94, 101, 143, 144
Comedy of Errors, 3, 5, 6, 44, 76, 84, 92, 100–2, 111, 114, 143
Coriolanus, 75, 78, 79, 89, 108, 138, 144
Cymbeline, 2, 33, 64, 74, 84, 85, 87, 101–103, 105, 110, 125, 138, 144
Hamlet, 23, 28, 29, 32, 33, 47, 48, 49, 63, 64, 73, 83, 86, 89, 90, 94, 105, 115, 119, 120–3, 127, 128, 139, 141, 143
Julius Caesar, 43, 77, 93, 95, 96, 134, 135, 145
1 King Henry IV, 56, 69, 73, 86, 94, 95, 120, 121
2 King Henry IV, 22, 43, 56, 67, 79, 91, 92, 100, 106, 119, 121, 122, 139
King Henry V, 30, 53, 56, 76, 77, 87, 90, 91, 108, 109, 118, 120, 121, 139, 144
1 King Henry VI, 3, 60, 76, 79, 91, 94, 100, 102, 108, 118, 138, 147, 149
2 King Henry VI, 3, 4, 5, 22, 34, 47, 84, 98, 103, 106, 107, 108, 114, 119, 124, 143, 147, 149
3 King Henry VI, 1, 3, 22, 53, 75, 76, 80, 84, 90, 103, 104, 109, 114, 127, 143, 146, 147, 149
King Henry VIII, 84, 85, 87, 99, 106, 109, 120
King John, 67, 74, 83, 100, 109, 115, 118, 143
King Lear, 43, 79, 87, 91, 96, 97, 99, 111, 125, 126, 127, 128, 143, 144
King Richard II, 2, 97, 115, 138, 143
King Richard III, 47, 65, 102, 105, 106, 107, 109, 114, 124, 135, 136, 146
Love's Labour's Lost, 56, 90, 93, 114, 119
Macbeth, 58, 80, 84, 89, 125, 133, 138, 139, 141, 144

Measure for Measure, 48

Merchant of Venice, 22, 47, 82, 84, 91, 97, 99, 101, 112, 114, 138, 139, 143

Merry Wives of Windsor, 56, 69, 84, 98, 101, 105, 106, 118, 119, 121

Midsummer Night's Dream, 91, 93, 114, 121, 139, 144

Much Ado About Nothing, 93, 94, 112, 143

Othello, 7–12, 23, 36, 42, 45, 55, 57, 77, 79, 80, 84, 93, 97, 100, 104, 107, 108, 112, 115, 116, 119, 125, 138

Pericles, 20–21, 24–27, 36, 40, 41, 48, 49, 61, 62, 63, 64, 79, 94, 101–3, 105–8, 114, 121, 125, 129, 131, 137, 139, 140, 143, 151, 152

Romeo and Juliet, 80, 81, 84, 109, 110, 118, 119

Taming of the Shrew, 97, 98, 99, 120

The Tempest, 36–40, 44, 46, 49, 54, 56–60, 63, 65, 71–75, 84, 86, 87, 88, 91, 101, 104–8, 110, 114, 124, 125, 133, 134, 135, 141, 153

Timon of Athens, 109, 125, 151

Titus Andronicus, 76, 97, 125, 138, 146

Troilus and Cressida, 43, 64, 74, 81, 94, 100, 102, 126, 138, 139, 143

Twelfth Night, 44, 45, 50, 51, 52, 54, 61, 74, 92, 94, 102, 106, 125, 139

Two Gentlemen of Verona, 32, 66, 76, 87, 139, 143

Winter's Tale, 33, 36, 42, 45, 73, 87, 91, 103, 110, 141

Poems:

Rape of Lucrece, 72, 74, 75, 81, 82, 90, 93, 119, 120, 125, 133, 138, 140, 146

Sonnets, 79, 90, 94, 102, 103, 114, 124, 146

Venus and Adonis, 33, 131, 137, 140

Shark, 139

Shelf, 82–85

Ship (types of), 97–102

Ship boy, 67

Shipwreck, 44–46, 83, 129

Shoal, 82–85

Short introduction . . . Swimming, A, 133, 134

Shoulder, 115

Shrouds, 40, 109

Shylock, 83

Sicily, 142

Signs of the weather, 140, 141

Simois, 125

Sinon, 120

Sky, 42, 43; *see also* Signs of the weather

Smith, Captain John, 54

Soldiers, 68

Solstice, 95, 141

Sounding, 86–88

"Sound off", "sound out", 19

Southampton (Hampton), 30

Southampton, Earl of, 49

Spain, 15, 35, 52, 86, 100, 147, 148

Spaniards, xiii, 8, 9, 17, 28, 29, 46 (cruelty of); 50, 72, 98, 104, 112, 117

Spheres, 94

Spieghel der Zeevaerdt, xiv

Spindrift, 124

Split, 39, 41, 44, 45

Squadron of the Watch, 19

Squalls, xvi, 143

St. Andrew, 112, 113

St. Elmo's fire, 39, 40

St. Matthew, 113

Stand, The, 74

Stars, 93–96

Steer, 107

Stem, 41, 42, 108

Stephano, 45, 50, 56, 65, 107, 135

Stern, 41, 42, 108

Sternage, 108

Storme, The, 36

Storms, 8, 9, 35–43, 110

Stow, John, 23

Strachey William, 42

Stratagem, 8, 48

Strategy, 11, 14, 121

Strike sail, etc., 22, 115, 116

Striking topmasts, 38

Stuff, 106

Succour ships, 26, 27

Suffolk, Duke of, 4, 5, 107, 119

Summers, Sir George, 40

Sunrise, 95

Sunset, 95

Surge, 125

Surgeon, 61–62

Swabber, 56, 60, 61

Swan, 76, 138

"Swell", 74
Swimming, 133–5
Sycorax, 73

Tack, 115
Tackle, 109
Tackling, 109
Talbot, 102
Tall ship, 39, 83, 97
Tanner, J. R., xvi
Technical language, *see* Sea terms
Tempest, 36
Tenison, E. M., xii
Thaliard, 121
Thames, xii, 28, 82, 84, 87, 98, 132
Thersites, 64
Three Voyages (Frobisher's), 123
Tide, 73–77
Tiger, 51, 58
Tilbury, 70
Timbers, 108
Timon of Athens, 109, 151
Titus Andronicus, 43
Tomb by the shore, 151
Topgallant, 110
Topmast, 38, 105, 110
Topsail, 20, 37, 59
Touchstone, 64, 90
Tractatus de Globis, 91
Trafalgar, 58
Treatise concerning the navie, A, 82, 98
Trinculo, 45, 71, 72, 135, 141
Trinity House, 78, 79, 80
Trinkermen, 132
True Repertory of the Wracke, 42
Trumpeter, 60
Try, 38
Tudor and Stuart Library, 1
Turks, 7, 8, 9, 55, 97
Types of ship, 97–102
Tyre; 20, 21

Ulysses, 43
Ursa Major, 93, 94, 95
Ursa Minor, 90, 93, 94

Vail, 112, 113, 116
Valdes, 49
Vanguard, H.M.S., 36
Vaux, W. S. W., 40
Venice, xi, 101
Venus, 91
Vere, Sir F., 8
Victory, H.M.S., 58, 111
Viola, 61, 106
Voyages and Travels (An English Garner), 35, 54
Voyages and Works of John Davis, 92

Waft, 3
Wagenaer, Lucas J., xiv
Waist, 105, 108
Walsingham, xiii, 8, 57
Wandering stars, 94
Ward, John, xiv
Warships, 97–99
Warwick, Earl of, 22
Wash, The, 74
Wash overboard, 41
Waterfowl, 135, 137, 138
Watergalls, 140
Waters, David W., xiv
Waterspouts, 126
Waves, 124–5
Westminster, 130, 137
Whale, 138, 139, 140
Whitmore, Walter, 4
Wight, Isle of, 29, 113
Wildfire, 120
Winchester, Bishop of, 108
Wind, 142, 143 (terms connected with)
Windward tide, 75
Wolsey, Cardinal, 84, 85, 87
World Encompassed, The, 40, 53
Worship, 65
Wright, Edward, xv, 35, 36, 92

Yards, 41, 105, 109, 111, 114
Yaw, 107, 12